Daily Mail

MONEY MAIL SAVERS' GUIDE 1992–1993

CHAPMANS

Chapmans Publishers Ltd
141–143 Drury Lane
London WC2B 5TB

First published by Chapmans
for Associated Newspapers Ltd 1992

ISBN 1-85592-735-7

Photoset in Linotron Plantin by
MC Typeset Ltd, Wouldham, Rochester, Kent
Printed in Great Britain by Benham and Company Limited

CONTENTS

CHAPTER ONE

Why save?

Nearly everyone saves at some point in his or her life if only for fairly obvious reasons, such as a deposit for a house, paying for a daughter's wedding or a new car.

Other people, even if they have no particular objective in mind, have a more or less continuous savings programme setting money aside on either a regular or more intermittent basis.

The Victorians identified it as the virtue thrift and although the nineteenth century connotations no longer apply – we don't need the protection of savings to avoid, at all costs, the fate of the workhouse – saving is still a good habit to acquire.

In the broadest possible terms, the money will always come in handy and, more importantly, it is a failsafe – should an emergency or personal disaster occur. Saving cannot prevent either happening, but it can alleviate some of the worst side effects.

But a vague appreciation that savings are "a good thing" is not really enough. To make the most of the very many different forms of savings and investment that are available, you do some preliminary fact-finding – about you.

For example, do you know exactly what your income is, let alone your after tax income? Do you know how much income you can expect in retirement? Are you panic-stricken at the thought of investment losing value? Do you even know what you want from your savings? Many people, it must be admitted, are a little woolly about the financial facts of life.

To help you decide (a) what you need from your savings and (b) the strategy to help you obtain it, answer the following basic questions.

Can I afford to save?

If the answer to this question and the next four questions is "No", then you have problems. Some, such as long term unemployment where savings can almost be a positive disadvantage, may be intractable. (Income Support is only available in full for those with savings of £3,000 or less, with scaled down benefits for those with savings up to £8,000. For housing benefit and poll tax benefit the ceiling is £16,000.) Others may be just a matter of making life-style adjustments.

Use the family budget planner on page 8 to work out just exactly where your disposable income goes. There are some interesting cost comparisons per month on page 7. Each individual and family must decide their own priorities, but it is important that you can answer "yes" to the next four questions.

Have I "rainy day" or emergency savings?

Advance notice is not given for most emergencies: the car clutch goes; the cistern bursts or a close member of your family working abroad becomes seriously ill. Can you afford the costs involved?

Before you begin any fancy footwork with exciting new investments such as new share issues, or even opt for higher interest on savings locked away for a longer time, make sure you have sufficient savings which are *immediately* available (or at the most can be withdrawn within two days).

The amount you need to save will vary from individual to individual, family to family. It should be £100–£300 at the very least and £500 is not too much for a single person. Married couples should think in terms of £1,000–£2,000 minimum. See Chapter Seven for more detailed analysis of suitable rainy day savings.

Will my family be financially protected should I die or be permanently unable to work?

Mortgage payments, HP commitments, food costs, electricity bills and school fees (to mention but a few of the family's outgoings) won't stop if you die.

Life assurance (see pages 61–8) is the principal means of making sure that your family or other dependants, such as elderly parents, will have financial security in the event of your death.

The cheapest form of life assurance, a good value-for-money buy is *term assurance* – however, it is not included here because it has no investment content. It pays out only in the event of the policyholder's death. The cost is around £16.50–£17.50 a month for a 29 year old man wanting £75,000 of cover for 25 years. Nor are the policies which cover you against sickness or accident included here.

- ☐ How much life insurance cover? As a very rough guide, think in terms of up to five times earnings. But don't forget that if you have
- ☐ *An endowment mortgage* – this will repay the house loan
- ☐ Or belong to a *company pension scheme* – you might have death cover up to four times salary built into the scheme. Should you leave that pension scheme that benefit will disappear, unless you join a similar scheme.

Am I satisfied with my present living accommodation?

If you are renting a flat or house, or sharing with your parents, the answer will probably be "No". In which case you need to start saving, hard, for your own home, and to get your feet on the housing ladder. It is sometimes possible to obtain 100 per cent home loans, but it is still wise to save (see Chapter Seven).

- ☐ It will get you in the habit of setting aside a large sum each month; otherwise you might find these monthly mortgage payments a bit of a shock.
- ☐ If you have a deposit, you might not have to pay the one-off premium of a mortgage guarantee insurance policy which lenders require on loans above 70–85 per cent of the house price.
- ☐ Legal fees, moving expenses and furnishings will eat away into any savings, even if you don't need or wish for a deposit.

Am I saving enough for my retirement?

To a certain extent *all* of your savings can be described, ultimately, as being for your retirement.

But there will be many other calls and temptations on your funds between now and then, so it is important to have some savings and investments which are not only specifically earmarked for retirement, but cannot be taken except as a pension.

Chapter Seven looks at this subject in more detail; and at the ways of improving your retirement income if you feel that, hitherto, you have been a little lax in respect of this essential saving.

WHY SAVE?

	Cost per month
● Twenty filter-tip cigarettes a day at £2.02 a pack	£56.56
● Shampoo and set at £7 a week	£28.00
● Two pints of beer a day at £1.30 a pint	£72.80
● Cat food at £2.80 a week	£11.20
● Two weekly magazines at 50p per week	£4.00
● Pocket money for 14–16 year olds at £3.30 per week (Wall's pocket money survey)	£13.20
● Mortgage protection plan for 25 years for 35 year old man per £25,000 house loan	£7.75
● Unit trust monthly savings plan	£25.00
● Minimum holding in National Savings Certificates	£25.00
● Bank and building society account can be opened for as little as	£1–£5

Money Mail – Budget planner

OUTGOINGS PER MONTH
Unavoidable expenditure

FOOD	£ ______
HOUSING	
Mortgage/rent .	£ ______
Ground rent .	£ ______
Water rates . .	£ ______
Poll tax . . .	£ ______
HEATING	
Electricity . .	£ ______
Gas	£ ______
Other fuel etc .	£ ______
INSURANCE	
Contents . . .	£ ______
Building . . .	£ ______
Life assurance .	£ ______
Motor	£ ______
Mortgage protection . .	£ ______
Other	£ ______
TRAVEL	
Season ticket .	£ ______
Car tax	£ ______
Maintenance payments . .	£ ______
Child care . .	£ ______
Other	£ ______
TOTAL	£ ______

SAVINGS

PAY poll tax and water rates by instalments. PAY bills together through Giro to save postage and bank charges. PAY car tax for full year. COMBINED house and buildings insurance can be cheaper. BUY the longest season ticket possible. INSULATE the house for substantial saving on energy bills. TURNING down the thermostat 4°F can save 10 per cent on heating bills. CHECK out school shop for second hand school clothes. BUY own brand food.

TAX TIPS

KEEP mortgage to £30,000 for maximum tax relief. BE wary of switching to another lender if your existing mortgage covers home improvements made before 6 April 1988. You could lose tax relief on this part of the new loan. CHECK your PAYE notice of coding (sent in January and February) to make sure all the allowances to which you are entitled are there. HIGHER rate taxpayers and people with income from other sources should check their Schedule E Notice of Assessment which explains how the Revenue has worked out your tax bill. If you disagree, appeal within 30 days.

DON'TS

DON'T buy gas, electricity or telephone stamps, but put money into building society. DON'T pay for gas or electricity through a slot meter. DON'T heat unused rooms. DON'T over-insure. DON'T cash in life insurance policy early; surrender values are poor. DON'T cash in life insurance bought before March 1984; you will lose valuable tax relief. NEVER pay in advance if you can pay in arrears.

OUTGOINGS PER MONTH
Other essentials

Petrol
other fares . . £ ______
TV licence . . £ ______
School fees/
clothes . . . £ ______
Pension
contributions . £ ______
Telephone . . £ ______
Garage repairs . £ ______
Medical/
Dentist . . . . £ ______
LOANS
HP . . . . . £ ______
Personal Loan . £ ______
Overdraft . . . £ ______

TOTAL £ ______

SAVINGS

TELEPHONE during cheap rate period. PAY regular bills by standing order, better still direct debit, to save postage. SEARCH out interest-free credit offers. OVERDRAFT is cheaper than a personal loan if you can get one. DRIVE carefully to conserve petrol. CONVERT your car to unleaded petrol, it's cheaper. PAY school fees in advance: can be 40 per cent cheaper. ALWAYS check for hidden charges in any credit deal. CHECK bank statements thoroughly. LIMIT directory enquiry calls (now 43.5p a time) or use a payphone which still allows free directory enquiries. CONVERT your current account to one which pays interest.

TAX TIPS

TAKE out as large a pension as you can afford. A pension-linked mortgage, with tax relief on the mortgage interest (up to £30,000 of loan) and pension contributions, is very tax efficient.

DON'TS

DON'T borrow money to pay off debts. DON'T go into the red without consulting your bank manager; bank charges on unauthorised borrowings are high. BANK budget accounts cost; organise your own system. DON'T spend money wrongly credited to your account; it has to go back. DON'T raise a loan on trading checks; rates are astronomical.

Additional checks

Telephone charges:

Peak rate: Mon–Fri 9am to 1pm
Standard rate: Mon–Fri 8am to 9am
1pm to 6 pm
Cheap rate: Mon–Fri 6pm to 8am
Sat & Sun all day

Each unit is 4.2p (excluding VAT)
Local calls – within exchange
Peak: 57.5 seconds; standard: 80 seconds; cheap: 220 seconds.
Trunk calls (A Rate – up to 56.4 kilometres)
Peak: 27 seconds; standard: 36.15 seconds; cheap: 80.8 seconds.
Trunk calls (B Rate – over 56.4 kilometres)
Peak: 23.95 seconds; standard: 32 seconds; cheap: 50.35 seconds.

Overdraft interest:

Your bank manager will almost invariably suggest a bank personal loan – which costs more than an overdraft. What is more, the interest rate is fixed for the duration of the loan, irrespective of what might happen to interest rates. Discuss your credit arrangements with him/her. Most managers will probably accede to your request for an overdraft. Then negotiate for the interest rate: overdraft rates range from 2½ per cent to 6 per cent over bank base rates. Most customers

OUTGOINGS PER MONTH
Important costs

HOUSEHOLD	
Kitchen equipment	£
Cleaning and toiletries	£
Hairdressing	£
Decorating	£
Birthday, Xmas presents	£
Holidays	£
Evening classes	£
Pocket money	£
Garden tools	£
Trade union fees	£
Vet	£
TV rental	£
School trips	£
Other	£
TOTAL	£

will be fobbed off with 5 per cent: persuade your bank manager to go lower.

One of the cheapest forms of overdraft credit is available to holders of "Gold" cards – the up-market charge or credit cards which have a built-in automatic overdraft facility of up to £10,000 (in most cases).

SAVINGS

BUY in bulk if there is room for storage. SEARCH out grants wherever these might be available; they are free gifts. CHECK your credit card terms: balance a flat initial fee with a lower interest rate (suitable if you use the credit regularly) against no fee and a higher interest rate. INSURE pets when they are young to cover later vet's bills. SOME subscriptions offer discount for paying by direct debit. USE customer discount cards where available.

TAX TIPS

USE child's tax relief allowance wherever possible; have money gifts made direct to child. CHILDREN can earn up to £3,445 a year before paying tax.

DON'TS

DON'T rent household equipment, televisions, video recorders and compact disc players; it's cheaper to buy. This includes telephones, but make sure you buy one that has been approved for connection to British Telecom lines – it will carry a green circle.

Pensions 1:
Many self-employed are wary about tying up the maximum possible into their private pension arrangements despite the attractive element of tax relief built into such schemes. Pension fund monies cannot be released (as a pension or permitted cash commutation) until stated retirement age. However, it is always possible to activate the pension plan "loan back" arrangements should an urgent need for cash emerge in the meantime.

Pensions 2:
Anyone not belonging to a company pension scheme can get tax relief up to 17.5 per cent of net relevant earnings (more once you are 36). If you haven't paid the maximum allowed in any of the previous six tax years, you can top up those contributions and obtain tax relief for those years.

OUTGOINGS PER MONTH
Flexible costs

Clothes . . .	£ _____
Furnishing . .	£ _____
Magazines and newspapers .	£ _____
Cosmetics . .	£ _____
Postage and stationery . .	£ _____
Garden . . .	£ _____
Laundry . . .	£ _____
Xmas entertainment .	£ _____
Credit cards . .	£ _____
Savings . . .	£ _____
TOTAL	£ _____

Direct debits:
Not only are some subscriptions cheaper if you pay by direct debit, but you might also save money if payments are debited from your account this way rather than by paying for the bills with more expensive-to-handle (from the bank's point of view) cheques as some banks still charge more for cheque withdrawals. Of course, this charge only applies if your account is not in credit – free banking, although not universally available, with the majority of bank accounts applies when the account is in the black.

SAVINGS

LEARN a money-making skill at evening classes. SHOP at sale times. BE cheeky and ask for discount for cash wherever appropriate. DUAL pricing is now allowed; pay by cash if it is cheaper than using a credit card. PAY credit card bill in full every month to avoid interest charges; some cards now charge interest from the purchase date if the account is not cleared that month. AVOID store cards which usually have a higher interest rate than bank credit cards. PAY store cards, if you insist on using them, by direct debit if you can't repay in full, as the interest charge is often lower. This is the case with some credit cards too.

TAX TIPS

HIGHER rate taxpayers should look for tax-free investments such as National Savings certificates, Tessas and PEPs (see individual sections for details). NON-taxpayers should go for investments that pay interest gross and register to receive interest without deduction of tax (otherwise it will be paid and a time interval will occur before the tax can be reclaimed). A wife's investment income can now be offset against her personal tax allowance so a non-working wife's savings should be in gross paying investments to "use up" her personal allowance. Since April 1991 banks and building societies have been able to pay interest gross to non-taxpayers.

DON'TS

DON'T buy clothes that can't go in the washing machine; dry cleaning costs are high. DON'T use store cards when their interest charges are higher than others.

Company loans:
Cheap or interest-free company loans, for example, to buy a season ticket could result in a higher tax bill. The Inland Revenue counts it as a taxable benefit assessing the value according to the "official rate of interest" applied to the loan.

OUTGOINGS PER MONTH
Desirable costs

Charity donations . .	£ ______
Eating out . .	£ ______
Cinema and theatre . . .	£ ______
Alcohol and tobacco . . .	£ ______
Hobbies/sport .	£ ______
Toys	£ ______
Books	£ ______
Records/tapes .	£ ______
Gambling . . .	£ ______
Office collections . .	£ ______
TOTAL	£ ______

SAVINGS

SOME theatres and cinemas sell half-price seats on Mondays. MATINEE performances are cheaper and less crowded. PENSIONER price concessions are often available. SET menus offer far better value than à la carte.

TAX TIPS

MAKE charitable donations under covenant or the gift aid scheme (for lump sums) for tax advantage. CONSIDER using a credit card which makes donations to named charities related to the amount cardholders spend. GAMBLING winnings are tax free.

DON'TS

DON'T sell any valuables to doorstep hawkers; get comparative valuations. DON'T spend needlessly on children.

Provided the interest worked out on this formula does not exceed £200, no tax will be charged: if it is £201 or more you will be taxed on the full amount, not just the excess over £200.

The official rate of interest is currently 10.5 per cent: this triggers off interest of just under £200 on a loan of £1,900.

Consolidation loans:
It is tempting to take out a consolidation loan to take care of all existing debts, but many debts – such as gas, electricity and telephone bills – are renewed every few months. As a rule of thumb, the borrowing term should not exceed the life span of the asset you are buying. For example, cars are renewed every two to three years; holidays come round once a year; electricity and other service bills once a quarter. Tailor your borrowing accordingly so that you have repaid one loan before the next one is taken out.

Interest-free credit:
Although this is valuable, do make sure that the store or shop which is offering it is not charging a price at the upper end of scale. With hi-fi and some "white" goods, the prices in discount stores might be sufficiently attractive to outweigh a temporary interest charge or loss of interest if you mobilise savings to buy them. Shopping around can be both tedious, time-consuming and only marginally beneficial: sometimes – and with these kind of goods in particular – it can be very worthwhile.

Rented equipment:
If you still prefer to rent your TV and similar equipment, keep an eye on the tariff and standard of equipment currently offered by the renter. You might be paying a rate, fixed some time ago, on equipment which is now let for a lower rental, or could "swap" your CD and video recorder, say, for a more comprehensive system for the same price.

CHAPTER TWO

From safety first to high risk

The difference between savings and investment is that the former is safer than investment which will always involve some element of risk. Understanding the risk spectrum from "safety first" to "high risk" is an important aspect of managing one's money well and deciding the most appropriate savings strategy (see Chapter Eight).

To help readers of *Money Mail Savers' Guide* we have devised a ratings guide which identifies the degree of investment risk that different kinds of savings and investment have.

Money Mail Rating

Safe *****

Sound ****!

Opportunity **!!!

Aggressive *!!!!

Risky !!!!!

It is an at-a-glance ratings symbol which gives readers a quick guide to the kind of investment they might be contemplating. The second half of this book, which goes through each investment one-by-one, uses this rating.

The qualities which determine an investment's risk are whether the capital value is fixed or varies; whether the rate of interest is fixed; the currency; whether the investment is narrowly or widely spread; and the market for those investments.

So the spectrum ranges from National Savings Certificates to unquoted foreign companies.

The various investment categories are:

- **Fixed capital, fixed interest**
- **Fixed capital, variable interest**
- **Variable capital, fixed interest**
- **Variable capital, variable interest**
- **Variable capital, variable interest, variable currency**
- **Variable capital, no interest**

Fixed capital, fixed interest

This type of investment is the safest of all. The investor knows, at any time, exactly what he will obtain from his money.

In this category are:

Bank, Deposit Taker and Offshore
Term Accounts
Tax Exempt Special Savings Account

Life Insurance
Guaranteed Growth & Income Bonds – provided held to maturity
School Fees Educational Trust
Annuity

Local Authority
Loans
Corporation Stock } provided they are held to maturity
Yearling Bond } provided they are held to maturity

National Savings
Capital Bonds
Income Bonds
Investment Account
Ordinary Account
37th Issue National Savings Certificates
Yearly Plan

Stock
Government fixed interest – provided held to maturity
Money Mail Rating *****

Fixed capital, variable interest

This form of investment is very safe, because the investor can always get his original capital back in full, even though the rate of interest it earns may vary.

In this category are:

Bank and Deposit Takers
- Deposit Account
- Children's Account
- High Interest Cheque Account
- High Interest Deposit Account
- Monthly Savings Account
- Notice Account
- Tax Exempt Special Savings Account

Building Society
- Cash Card Account
- Cheque Book Account
- Children's Account
- Instant Access Account
- Monthly Income
- Monthly Savings Account
- Offshore
- Share Account
- Tax Exempt Special Savings Account
- Term Share

Life Insurance
- With-Profits Endowment – provided held to maturity
- With-Profits Flexible – provided held to guaranteed surrender dates

National Savings
- Index-Linked Certificates
- Premium Bonds

Offshore
- High Interest Cheque Account

Pensions
- Additional Voluntary Contributions
- Transfer Plan

Money Mail Rating *****

Variable capital, fixed interest

Such investment is moving out of the very safe category. Although the interest remains fixed, there can be wide fluctuations in capital values, leaving the investor hopefully better off, but maybe worse off, therefore not suitable for emergency funds. In this category are:

Variable capital, fixed
- Government and Local Authority Stock – unless held to redemption
- Company Loan and Debenture Stock – unless held to redemption
- Preference Shares

Money Mail Rating ****! *to* **!!!

Variable capital, variable interest

This covers a very wide range of share investments, with different degrees of risk which depend upon the size, track record, marketability of individual shares in different companies, and whether or not the investment is widely spread, to narrow the risk, over the range of shares. But they are all risk investments in which an investor can see his capital dwindle, occasionally disappear, and his income suffer the same fate.

Shares
Companies listed on the Stock Exchange, including Personal Equity Plans.
Money Mail Rating ****! *to* *!!!!

Smaller and younger companies with shares quoted on the Stock Exchange's own Unlisted Securities Market.
Money Mail Rating **!!! *to* !!!!!

Investment Trusts
including Personal Equity Plans

Unit Trusts
including Personal Equity Plans

Money Mail Rating ****! *to* *!!!!

Life Assurance
Investment Bonds
Unit-Linked Savings
Money Mail Rating ****! *to* *!!!!

Variable capital, variable interest, variable currency

Currencies rise and fall in value against each other, and investments which have to get the currency right as well as the underlying investments have a high risk factor. Investment managers admit that selecting the right currency and "hedging" (to minimise the risk) is one of their most difficult tasks.

Offshore
Currency Funds
Unit Trusts
Money Mail Rating **!!! *to* !!!!!

Variable capital, no interest

Investments such as commodities, precious metals, antiques which may not be easily marketable
Gold
Offshore funds investing in alternative investments
Money Mail Rating *!!!! *to* !!!!!

CHAPTER THREE

Tax and savings

If the most fundamental reasons for saving are *emergencies*, *family protection*, *house purchase* and *provision for old age*, the most significant feature underlying your savings and investment decisions after assessing the *risk factor* is *tax*, which affects the return you get on your investments.

Some forms of investment and savings are more suitable for higher rate taxpayers; others will be of more benefit to those who pay little or no tax.

Both income and capital gains are now taxed at the same rates: either 25 per cent or 40 per cent. Capital gains tax liabilities sit on top of income, and could push you into the 40 per cent bracket if your *total* taxable income plus taxable gains exceeds £23,700.

To make the most of the wide variety of savings discussed in greater detail later, it is sensible to get to grips with the tax system and how it affects you, and your family.

Income tax

Contrary to general myth we don't pay tax on all our income. Everyone, from the youngest baby in the country to the oldest pensioner, is entitled to some tax-free income (assuming, of course, that they have some income). In addition, some state benefits are tax free, some expenditure is given tax relief and the interest on certain forms of savings is tax free.

The principal tax-free *allowances* vary according to marital status and age, and whether you are a single parent family (see tax table below).

Certain outgoings are given tax relief up to a certain amount. These include:

- ☐ mortgage interest relief at basic rate of tax only (since 6 April 1991) on home loans up to £30,000;
- ☐ pension scheme contributions of up to 15 per cent of your earnings if employed, or 17½ per cent if self-employed or not in a company pension scheme, rising with a personal pension plan to 20 per cent at age 36 and increasing to a maximum of 40 per cent at age 61 and over, qualify for tax relief at your top rate of tax. (From age 36 contributions are less generous for the old-style retirement annuities.) Members of company pension schemes who joined after 1 June 1989 will be restricted to tax relief on pension scheme contributions on earnings up to £75,000 only. The same limits apply to personal pension plans taken out since 6 April 1989.
- ☐ maintenance and alimony payments made before 15 March 1988 are given tax relief; on agreements made from 15 March 1988 relief is given up to a limit equal to the difference between the single and married person's allowance;
- ☐ covenanted payments to charities attract tax relief at basic and higher rate tax.
- ☐ life assurance policies taken out before 13 March 1984 qualify for tax relief at 12½ per cent.
- ☐ payroll deductions to charity up to maximum donation of £50 a month qualify for tax relief.
- ☐ individual gifts to charity over £600 are tax free. Gifts are paid net of basic rate tax; higher rate tax relief is claimed by the taxpayer.

Income and savings which are exempt from income tax are:

TAX AND SAVINGS

Income Tax rates

Taxable Income £		Rate %	Tax Payable £
1992–93	0– 2,000	20	400
	2,000–23,700	25	5,425
	over 23,700	40	
1991–92	0–23,700	25	5,925
	over 23,700	40	
		1990–91	**1989–90**
Additional rate (discretionary trusts)		10	10

Income Tax allowances

	1992–93 £	1991–92 £
Personal	3,445	3,295
Married couple*	1,720	1,720
Additional personal and widow's bereavement	1,720	1,720
Personal (65–74)	4,200	4,020
Married couple (65–74)*	2,465	2,355
Personal (75 plus)	4,370	4,180
Married couple (75 plus)*	2,505	2,395
Blind person's**	1,080	1,080
Age allowance income limit†	14,200	13,500

* This is in addition to the personal allowance which *each* spouse receives; in the first instance it is given to the husband.

† Once income exceeds £14,200 the age allowance is reduced by £1 for every £2 of income until it reaches the level of the normal allowances. The extra personal allowance runs out at £15,710 (age 65–74) or £16,050 (75 plus); for the partner claiming the married couple's allowance at £17,200 (65–74) or £17,620 (75 plus).

** Reduced by any tax-free disability benefit received.

- ☐ National Savings Bank Ordinary Account – the first £70 of interest a year;
- ☐ National Savings Certificates (index-linked as well as conventional);
- ☐ National Savings Yearly Plan – the interest;
- ☐ Premium Bond prizes;
- ☐ Save As You Earn (SAYE) bonuses;
- ☐ Personal Equity Plan – dividends, whether they are reinvested or distributed;
- ☐ Tax Exempt Special Savings Accounts (Tessa) – tax free if held for five years; if income is withdrawn earlier it is paid net; the tax withheld is paid as a tax-free bonus after five years.
- ☐ Life assurance policies – the proceeds of qualifying policies (usually where regular payments are in force) paid out either at death or after 7½–10 years;
- ☐ Annuities – a proportion of the annuity income which varies with age;

- ☐ Football pools – the winnings; and other betting winnings (although you may have to pay betting tax).
- ☐ Maintenance payments – on agreements made from 15 March 1988.
- ☐ Redundancy payments – up to £30,000.

Benefits which are not taxable and should not be entered on your tax return include:
Child benefit
Mobility allowance
One parent benefit
Guardian's allowance and child's special allowance
Income support
Industrial disablement benefits
Severe disablement allowance
Christmas bonus paid with state pension or allowance
Child dependency additions
Family credit
Sickness benefit
Housing benefit
Attendance allowance
Social fund payments
Maternity allowance
Invalidity benefit
Widow's payment

Pensions which are non-taxable and should not be entered on your tax return include:
War widows' pension
Certain pensions for wounds or disability caused or aggravated by military service or for other war injuries
Pensions paid to victims of Nazi persecution by German or Austrian government should be entered, although special provisions apply.

Grants which are non-taxable and should not be entered on your tax return include:
Assisted places grant
Student grant

Working out your tax bill

Basic rate is only levied on your *taxable income*: this is your income after deducting your allowances and permitted outgoings and ignoring, of course, tax-free income.

There is a new reduced rate band of 20 per cent on the first £2,000 of income. Basic rate tax is currently 25 per cent on taxable income between £2,000 and £23,700; anything over that is taxed at 40 per cent.

There are 25 million taxpayers, of whom 1,800,000 pay higher rate tax.

Pensioners who are reliant on the state retirement pension only are unlikely to be taxpayers, but need to be very careful that modest savings which are taxed at source don't tip them into the basic rate tax bracket (see Chapter Five).

Trust income

Using trusts for both convenience and tax planning has a long history. There are basically three kinds of trust: income in possession trusts, discretionary, and accumulation and maintenance trusts.

Interest in possession trusts, which give the beneficiary the right to the trust income, are widely used for inheritance tax planning as the lifetime gift to the trust is a PET – that is a potentially exempt transfer. Provided the settlor survives seven years after making the gift, it will pass beyond the inheritance tax net (see page 22). The beneficiary pays income tax at his or her appropriate tax rate.

The beneficiary of a discretionary trust does not have the automatic right to income; as the name indicates, it is at the discretion of the trustee. This affects the tax treatment of the income. There is a special rate of tax for discretionary trusts which is basic rate tax (25 per cent) plus an additional rate (10 per cent), making a combined total of 35 per cent.

If the income is distributed to a child or other non-taxpayer, the 35 per cent tax paid can be reclaimed. With a child, use tax form R232 to reclaim the tax. However, if the parent has settled the gift, the child's trust income will be aggregated with his own.

Accumulation and maintenance trusts, used often to provide school fees, work in a similar way. It is quite possible that the income will not be distributed immediately, in which case the trustees will pay the 35 per cent tax on the trust fund's income. This can then be paid out later as capital without a further charge to tax.

The big difference between discretionary and accumulation and maintenance trusts is in respect of inheritance tax. Gifts into the former are not PETs, but are subject to inheritance tax, but at the reduced lifetime rate of 20 per cent. Gifts into the latter trust, provided the settlor survives seven years, are exempt from inheritance tax.

Trusts are very useful for helping with estate and tax planning where substantial sums could be involved. It costs £300–£500 to set up a trust.

CHAPTER FOUR

Capital taxes

Income tax isn't the only tax you must consider; the capital taxes – capital gains tax and inheritance tax (formerly capital transfer tax) – can have some bearing on your investment decisions.

Capital gains tax

If you make a profit when you sell an asset (or indeed give it away for more than its acquisition value) then you have made a capital gain. Conversely, you might have a capital loss on your hands if the asset has decreased in value before you sell or part with it.

In each tax year capital gains, less capital losses and any expenses incurred in buying and selling (such as legal fees or commission) are, if this exceeds a certain level, subject to capital gains tax at either 25 per cent or 40 per cent. Your taxable gains are aggregated with your income to determine which rate you pay (see Chapter Three).

There are several comforting facts to remember about capital gains tax.

- ☐ Many types of assets are exempt from capital gains tax.
- ☐ Capital gains tax only applies to the *gains* you make, not the actual disposal price.
- ☐ The level at which the tax begins is sufficiently high – £5,800 in tax year 1992–93 – to keep many investors out of this tax net.
- ☐ Only gains accrued since 31 March 1982 will be taxable.
- ☐ The indexation of capital gains made since March 1982, which "increases" the purchase price of your asset in line with the rise in the retail price index, makes it even less likely that capital gains tax will apply.
- ☐ Capital losses can be offset against taxable gains, but can also, if not used in one tax year, be carried forward indefinitely to set against capital gains you might make in the future.
- ☐ No capital gains tax is paid at death: whoever inherits your assets does so at the market value at your death.

Principal assets exempt from capital gains tax

You will not have to pay capital gains tax on the disposal of the following assets.

Your principal home If you have more than one house you can select which is your main home provided the choice is made within three years of buying the second. You can subsequently change your mind, but can only back-date your choice by two years.

Your car

Your "chattels" – personal belongings such as furniture and jewellery sold for £6,000 or less; gallantry decorations you have earned, not bought, are totally exempt.

National Savings Certificates, Yearly Plan, Capital Bond, Save As You Earn (SAYE) and Premium Bond prizes.

British Government stock and company loan or debenture stock.

Legal tender (which still includes gold sovereigns, half sovereigns and the Britannia gold coins) and any foreign currency obtained for personal use abroad.

Personal Equity Plan

Tax Exempt Special Savings Accounts

Business Expansion Scheme shares held for qualifying five years.

Tangible movable property with a predictable life of no more than 50 years such as boats, caravans and animals.

Life insurance policies of which you are the original owner.

Gifts to charities or the nation.

Indexation of capital gains

Inflation, as opposed to real growth in the value of any assets you subsequently sell, is taken into account by linking the purchase price with the change in the Retail Price Index since then.

This has the effect of "increasing" the purchase price and thereby reducing or even eliminating your capital gain altogether. In the latter case, it has actually created a capital loss. By the same token indexation can increase an existing loss.

On post 31 March 1982 gains use the Retail Price Index for the appropriate month (see page 121) to work out the index-linked value which is to be added to your original purchase price.

For example, take shares bought in August 1984 for £3,000 and sold for £6,000 in January 1987. The Retail Price Index rose by 10.8 per cent between

Free tax leaflets from the Inland Revenue

Booklet no.	*Title*
IR1	Extra-statutory concessions
IR4	Income tax and Pensioners
IR4A	Income tax – Age Allowance
IR11	Tax Treatment of Interest Paid
IR13	Income Tax – Wife's Earnings Election
IR20	Residents and Non-Residents – Liability to tax in the United Kingdom
IR22	Income Tax – Personal Allowances
IR23	Income Tax and Widows
IR24	Class 4 National Insurance Contributions
IR28	Starting in Business
IR33	Income Tax and School Leavers
IR34	Income Tax – Pay As You Earn
IR41	Income tax and the Unemployed
IR42	Income Tax – Lay-offs and short-time work
IR43	Income Tax and Strikes
IR45	Income Tax, Capital Gains Tax and Capital Transfer Tax – What happens when someone dies
IR46	Income Tax and Corporation Tax – Clubs, Societies and Associations
IR51	Business Expansion Scheme
IR52	Your Tax Office – why it is where it is
IR56/N139	Employed or Self-Employed?
IR57	Thinking of working for yourself?
IR60	Income Tax and Students
IR63	MIRAS Mortgage Interest Relief at Source
IR65	Giving to Charity – how individuals can get tax relief
IR74	Deeds of Covenant – getting it right for tax
IR77	Taxation of Maintenance Payments
IR78	Personal Pension
IR80	Independent Taxation – A Guide for Married Couples

Booklet no.	*Title*
IR81	Independent Taxation – A Guide for Pensioners
IR82	Independent Taxation – A Guide for Husbands on a Low Income
IR85	BES schemes – Private Rented Housing
IR86	A Guide to Mortgage Interest for Married Couples
IR89	Personal Equity Plans (PEPs)
IR90	Independent Taxation – A Guide to Tax Allowances and Reliefs
IR91	Independent Taxation – A Guide for Widows and Widowers
IR92	Income Tax – A Guide for One-parent Families
IR93	Separation, Divorce and Maintenance Payments
IR95	Shares for Employees – Profit Sharing Schemes
IR97	Shares for Employees – SAYE Share Options
IR103	Tax Relief for Private Medical Insurance
IR110	Can you stop paying tax on your bank and building society interest?
IR111	How to claim a repayment of tax on bank and building society interest
IR112	How to claim a repayment of income tax
IR113	Gift Aid – A Guide for Donors and Charities
IR114	TESSA – Tax Free Interest for Taxpayers
CGT	Capital Gains Tax – An Introduction
CGT4	Capital Gains Tax – Owner-occupied Houses
CGT6	Capital Gains Tax – Retirement: Disposal of a business
CGT13	The Indexation Allowance for Quoted Shares
CGT 15	A Guide for Married Couples
IHT	Inheritance Tax

August 1984 and December 1986. As 10.8 per cent of £3,000 is £324 that amount of index-linked value must be added to your original purchase price of £3,000, bringing it to £3,324 and thus reducing the capital gain to £2,676.

Inheritance tax

Inheritance tax replaced capital transfer tax on 18 March 1986. It bears more resemblance to the old estate duty (which was itself replaced by capital transfer tax) in that only gifts at death (or near) are taxable.

Substantial exemptions from inheritance tax are allowed and in addition the first £150,000 of gifts or bequests is also exempt from the tax. The balance attracts tax at 40 per cent (other than lifetime gifts to discretionary trusts where the rate is 20 per cent).

However, substantial house price inflation means that many people who might hitherto have considered they had "little to leave" might find their estate liable to this tax.

All gifts made seven years before death are tax free. All non-exempt gifts made within three years of death are liable to inheritance tax and included in your estate. Gifts made between three and seven years are taxed on a sliding scale.

Inheritance tax rates from 6 April 1992

Portion of value £,000	On death* Rate of Tax
0–150	Nil
Over 150	40%

Inheritance tax rates from 6 April 1991

Portion of value £,000	On death* Rate of Tax
0–140	Nil
Over 140	40%

*Also applies to any gift made within three years of death.

Gifts exempt from inheritance tax

- ☐ Gifts between husband and wife.
- ☐ Gifts of £3,000 in each tax year; an unused portion can be brought forward one year.
- ☐ Wedding gifts: parents – £5,000 each; grandparents, great-grandparents and bride and groom to each other – £2,500; anyone else – £1,000.
- ☐ Any number of individual gifts not exceeding £250 (provided the recipient has not received gifts under the two previous headings).
- ☐ Money spent on your child's maintenance and education; reasonable provision for care of dependent relative.
- ☐ "Normal expenditure" gifts out of taxed income (*not* capital) the making of which does not affect your standard of living.
- ☐ Gifts to charities.
- ☐ Gifts to museums, art galleries and the National Trust including property of "outstanding national interest".

Gifts made within seven years of death

	% taxable
more than seven years before	0
more than six years before	20
more than five years before	40
more than four years before	60
more than three years before	80
less than three years before	100

CHAPTER FIVE

Tax treatment of your investments

With few exceptions, most forms of interest are taxable and must be declared on your tax return, even if basic rate tax has been deducted at source.

If you haven't been sent a tax return and have untaxed interest to declare, it is still your legal responsibility to declare it; ring up your tax office for a tax return.

Tax-free investments

Tax-free investments do not have to be declared on the tax return. Tax-free income includes interest on conventional and index-linked National Savings Certificates, National Savings Yearly Plan, SAYE and Premium Bond winnings. Interest on Tax Exempt Special Savings Accounts will be tax free if reinvested; if the income is withdrawn it will be paid net, but the tax withheld is paid as tax-free bonus after five years if the capital is not withdrawn before.

Tax-free income which does not have to be declared on your tax return are the dividends paid on investments in a Personal Equity Plan. There is no capital gains tax payable on the proceeds. Husband and wife can each take out one Personal Equity Plan each calendar year.

Tax-free income which does have to be declared on your tax return is the first £70 of interest from a National Savings Bank Ordinary Account. Husband and wife can each earn up to £70 a year tax free from their individual Ordinary Accounts.

The interest is declared on your tax return, because any excess over £70 which you might have earned from that account is taxable.

Bank, Building Society, Deposit Taker and Local Authority loan and interest

Since 6 April 1991 banks, building societies, deposit takers and local authorities in respect of their fixed term loans, all pay interest either without deduction of tax for those registered as non-taxpayers or with basic rate tax deducted at source.

It means that basic rate taxpayers have no further tax liability in respect of their investment, although it must still be declared on the tax return. However, higher rate taxpayers must pay higher rate taxes on the interest. Non-taxpayers who fail to register (forms are provided in bank and building society branches) will be able to reclaim the tax paid on their interest.

In respect of joint accounts where one partner pays tax and the other is a non-taxpayer, most building societies and some banks will pay half the interest net and the other half gross.

Older taxpayers of modest income who might qualify for Age Allowance, the extra tax relief given to those over 65, and more still to those over 75, should be careful with interest which comes "tax paid". On the tax return it has to be declared gross – that is, as though tax had not been deducted at source – in order to calculate one's total income. This is often overlooked when calculating whether or not one is entitled to the age allowance. Tax-free National Savings, such as Certificates, or Personal Equity Plans are a good investment for borderline incomes.

To gross up "tax paid" interest

Divide the tax paid interest by 75 and multiply by 100, e.g.

i) Net interest of £75

$$\frac{75}{75} \times 100 = £100 \text{ gross interest}$$

ii) Net interest of £100

$$\frac{100}{75} \times 100 = £133 \text{ gross interest}$$

Higher rate taxpayers must also gross up the tax paid interest to work out their extra tax liability, e.g.

i) Net interest of £75 = £100 gross
a 40% rate taxpayer must pay 15% tax (i.e. 40% – 25% the basic rate already paid) on that interest = £15 extra tax to be paid.
Net interest of £75 – £15 higher rate tax = interest net of 40% = £60.

ii) Net interest of £100 = £133 gross
a 40% rate taxpayer must pay 15% more tax (i.e. 40% – 25% basic rate already paid) on that interest = £20 extra tax to be paid.
Net interest of £100 – £20 higher rate tax = interest net of 40% = £80.

Inland Revenue check

Although the interest from all these forms of investment is tax paid (unless the saver is registered as a non-taxpayer), the institutions are obliged to notify the Inland Revenue where interest has been paid.

From 6 April 1992 all interest paid will be notified to the Inland Revenue. The limits in the tax year 1991–92 varied. In the case of the bank and deposit takers, the interest level was £500, building societies £1,400, local authorities £400. The National Savings Bank, which pays interest gross, notified the Inland Revenue when interest earned exceeded £250 on the Investment Account and £250 on the Ordinary Account. Gross interest in excess of £250 on other National Savings investments had to be notified.

National Savings Accounts, Government Stock (held on the National Savings Stock Register) and Offshore Investments which pay interest gross

The two National Savings Bank accounts (the Ordinary and Investment), National Savings Income Bonds, Government Stock bought from the National Savings Stock Register, War Loan, and interest from abroad is paid without deduction of tax – and these are therefore particularly appropriate forms of investment for non-taxpayers.

For taxpayers there are special rules for working out the tax on their gross interest, which depends on when they were bought. The tax is payable on 1 January of the year of assessment.

i) In the first tax year in which they are bought (tax years run from 6 April to the following 5 April), you are taxed on the actual interest you receive or have credited to you in that tax year. You declare the interest on your tax return for that year and will receive an assessment a few months later and be expected to pay the tax due within 30 days.

ii) In the second tax year, the same applies.

iii) In the third tax year, you are taxed on the interest you received in the *previous* year; or you can choose to pay tax on the interest you actually receive in that tax year (a worthwhile option if the interest is lower).

iv) In the fourth and subsequent years you pay tax on the interest you received in the previous year.

v) When you close an account, in that tax year you are charged tax on the actual interest you receive in that tax year.

vi) In the penultimate tax year, you normally pay tax on the previous year's interest (see iv above), but if you have by then closed the account, your tax assessment might be revised so that you pay tax on the actual interest received that year if it is higher.

If the amount of tax due is relatively small, the Inland Revenue might collect it by adjusting your PAYE tax code number downwards, instead of asking for a lump sum payment.

Life insurance policies

Although life insurance companies pay tax, which affects the position of their life funds (in which your money is placed), most life insurance policy proceeds – the sum you collect at maturity or death – are free of both income and capital gains tax. The capital gains tax that life offices have to pay on their life funds is reflected in the underlying value of the investments; or with some unit-linked policies, a deduction for capital gains tax might be made from the proceeds of a policy you encash.

With investment bonds, single premium insurance bonds, higher rate taxpayers may be liable to higher rate tax *only* on the proceeds; or on the proceeds of regular premium policy encashed before three-quarters of the original term has been reached or 10 years (whichever is less).

Up to 5 per cent of the original investment can be withdrawn as "income" from investment bonds with the tax liability deferred until the bond is encashed or 20 years, if earlier.

The objective for higher rate taxpayers is to defer the tax liability until a date when their tax rate will be lower. For both higher rate taxpayers and older taxpayers who are on the age allowance borderline, the attraction of such a plan is that the "income" does not have to be declared on the tax return.

"Top slicing relief" is applied when higher rate taxpayers encash their investment bonds to reduce the tax liability by taking into account the number of years the investment has been held.

Policyholders who took out regular premium policies before 13 March 1984 are still eligible for life assurance tax relief of 12½ per cent on the premiums. The relief is deducted from the premiums so that only the net amount is payable. Hang on to such policies, unless there are compelling reasons to stop paying.

Personal pensions

Self-employed and those not in an occupational pension scheme have for a long time been able to build up a pension entitlement for themselves with a self-employed retirement annuity, often known as Section 226 policies. These have been replaced by personal pension plans which are available to both the self-employed and employees who do not have a company pension scheme to join, or elect not to join or remain in a company pension scheme.

Tax relief, at your highest rate, is given on personal pension plan contributions up to an earnings limit of £75,000 for entrants from 6 April 1989 onwards at the following rates:

Up to age 35	17½%
Up to age 36–45	20%
Up to age 46–50	25%
Up to age 51–55	30%
Up to age 56–60	35%
61 and over	40%

In addition, employees can come out of the SERPS (the State Earnings Related Pension Scheme), and the Government will invest into your personal pension plan the relevant National Insurance "contracting out" rebates for both employer and employee (currently totalling 5.8 per cent but reducing to 4.8 per cent from 1993, plus a 1 per cent age related rebate for those over 30). A 2 per cent (of earnings) bonus is paid by the Government for each year up to 1993 for all people who come out of SERPS and into a personal pension plan.

Investment is made in a tax-free investment fund, managed by a life insurance company. Other institutions such as building societies and unit trust groups are providing personal pension plans too.

Pension investment is long term. Except for certain jobs with early "retirement" such as divers or croupiers, Section 226 cannot be taken, at the moment, until age 60; with personal pension plans retirement age can be as low as 50, but few people will have earned enough to take their pension so young. The latest you can retire is 75.

Although the pension itself will be taxable, part of the proceeds of a personal pension plan can be taken as a cash lump sum, but for policies taken out after 17 March 1987, that figure is limited to £150,000.

Late starters who have delayed their pension planning, can carry back up to six years pension plan contributions.

Provided you have set aside the maximum amount of contribution for the current year, you can then top up the preceding tax years' contributions for a total of six years, starting with the earliest relevant year. Tax relief is given at current tax rates.

With Section 226 policies the contribution ceilings are different. There is no earnings cap.

Up to age 50	17½%
Up to age 51–55	20%
Up to age 56–60	22½%
Up to age 61–75	27½%

For the relevant tax years 1982–83 to 1986–87 the contribution rates were based on the year in which you were born.

after 1933	17½%
1916–1933	20%
1914–1915	21%
1912–1913	24%
1910–1911	26½%
1908–1909	29½%
1907 or earlier	32½%

No tax relief is given on contributions made after age 75 years.

CHAPTER SIX

Savings and the family

There has been a revolution in the way in which families are taxed which has significant implications for the way in which we save money. Since 6 April 1990, a husband and wife have been treated as separate individuals, each with their own personal allowance. And irrespective of whether a wife's income is earned or unearned she is still able to set it against her personal allowance.

(Previously, a wife's unearned income was always, from a tax point of view, treated as belonging to her husband.)

It means that from now on, each partner in the marriage is able to enjoy tax-free income of £3,445 (the level of the new personal allowance). In addition, there is the married couple's allowance of £1,720 which, in the first instance, will go to the husband but which can be transferred to the wife if his income is insufficient.

In addition, each spouse is now entitled to their own capital gains tax exemption of the first £5,800 of gains in the year.

In order to maximise the family's income, it therefore makes sense to make full use of the wife's personal allowance – even if she is not working. The simplest way is to increase her savings so that she has investment income to offset against her allowance. Tax-free investments, which have hitherto been the most sensible form of investment for her, no longer fit the bill. She needs income which is either paid gross (that is before tax) or net, but on which she can reclaim any basic rate tax paid on her behalf.

For example why should she bother with a Tax Exempt Special Savings Account? She can obtain gross interest without tying up capital for five years, and she will not be able to offset the interest against her personal allowance. Similarly the tax-free income from a Personal Equity Plan will not help reduce her personal allowance.

With gross interest rates of 9–10 per cent, she can have savings of around £30,000 – and not pay tax on the interest. However, it must be from her money. If a husband gives his wife capital to invest in this tax efficient way, and the marriage subsequently fails, he cannot demand the money back. It will be hers.

Where a couple have savings in a joint name, the taxman will deem that half the interest belongs to the wife and half to the husband. If you don't want to split the income from a joint holding on a 50–50 basis, you must let the Inland Revenue know how you want it apportioned.

Investments for Non-Working Wives

- Building Society Accounts
- National Savings Investment Account
- National Savings Income Bonds
- High Yielding Unit Trusts
- High Yielding Investment Trusts

Investments not Suitable for a Non-Working Wife

- National Savings Certificates
- National Savings Yearly Plan
- Personal Equity Plans
- Tax Exempt Special Savings Account

Children

All children are potential taxpayers and entitled to the single person's tax allowances in respect of any interest they earn, with one important exception. As they are unlikely to be taxpayers, parents should register them as non-taxpayers to receive bank or building society interest gross. Grandparents cannot do this on behalf of their grandchildren.

Income from any money given by parent(s) is, apart from the first £100, treated as the donor parent's for tax purposes. State child benefit, saved for a child, counts as a gift of money from the parent.

The one exception to the rule is when money is given to the child "absolutely" in trust, and the income accumulated until the child is 18 or marries.

So children's savings fall into two categories with the following provisos.

The increase from £5 to £100 in the amount of tax-free income from parental gifts means that the first £1,000 of such savings (approximately) can be invested without tax considerations.

Interest on tax-free investments are sometimes so low that they compare unfavourably with net (after tax) returns elsewhere. Parents must decide which is more important: a lower tax bill for themselves, or a better return for their children. In such circumstances, the gift could come via a non-working mother who still has some of her own personal tax allowance to use up.

a) **savings from parental gifts**

This includes pocket money and child benefit invested on the child's behalf. The money should be in savings where the interest is tax free.

Building Society Children's Account

Bank Children's Account

Building Society Instant Access Account

National Savings Certificates

National Savings Children's Bonus Bond

b) **savings from all other sources**

This includes birthday gifts, savings from Saturday jobs and other cash windfalls. For greatest convenience, the money should be in savings where the interest is paid gross (see above).

National Savings Bank Investment Account

National Savings Children's Bonus Bonds

Government Stock on the National Savings Stock Register

Offshore bank accounts

Alternatively, children's money can be in investments, such as shares and unit trusts, where basic rate tax is deducted at source but can be reclaimed by non-taxpayers. Use Tax Claim (Form R232) to reclaim tax on behalf of a child.

Children need to learn about money management and sometimes the investment for long term savings which pays the most interest and has the most efficient tax structure, such as the National Savings Bank Investment Account (it requires one month's notice to withdraw funds) and the Children's Bonus Bond, might not be the most suitable for the week-to-week money transactions.

CHAPTER SEVEN

The essential savings

In Chapter One, we identified the four types of essential savings which all families should consider; single persons might be able to opt out of one of them – financial protection for dependants.

Emergency savings

You may get no advance warning when a financial emergency strikes, so you must have money easily available to meet those unexpected bills, out-of-the-blue demands on your pocket.

The only question is how large your emergency fund should be. To a certain extent this depends on your family circumstances. A family with a chronically sick child, for example, will almost certainly need a larger emergency fund; and the self-employed will fear the cash consequences of sickness more. If you are well placed to borrow money to meet emergencies, then you might prefer to have less in your immediate emergency fund.

Between £500 and £3,000 is a suitable amount for an emergency fund. As a rule of thumb, up to three months' pay is the amount a family should consider for its emergency fund. Higher earners can probably think in terms of less; young single persons, too, will probably reduce that target. For people of modest resources, an emergency fund might be their only form of saving. If you haven't got a lump sum to earmark for emergencies, set about building one up with regular savings which carry no penalties if you have to stop saving to draw on the fund.

Because it is a fund designed for emergencies, these savings must be accessible on demand and in full. This restricts the choice to a range of bank, building society, deposit taker and offshore accounts.

In addition, the physical convenience and networks of these institutions have to be taken into account. If your emergency fund is set at quite a high level, you need not have all of it at immediate notice. Seven day notice periods and even as long as a month's notice can be acceptable for the second tier of your emergency savings.

Do not forget that once your emergency fund has been tapped, it will either need replacing or topping up to the desired level. Bring back your second level of emergency savings to immediate access accounts, and then replace that level of savings from other sources.

Lump sum savings immediately available

Bank Deposit Account (small penalty)

Bank High Interest Cheque Account

Bank and Deposit Taker Savings Accounts

Building Society Instant Access (provided minimum balance maintained)

Building Society Ordinary Account

Offshore High Interest Cheque Account

Offshore Single Currency Fund

National Savings Ordinary Account

Lump sum savings available within a month

Bank High Interest Deposit Account

Bank and Deposit Taker Notice Account (some)

Building Society Notice Account (some)

National Savings Bank Investment Account

National Savings Certificates (small penalty)

National Savings Index-Linked Certificates

National Savings Premium Bond

Regular savings

Bank Monthly Savings Account

Building Society Monthly Savings Account

Tax Exempt Special Savings Account (Tessa) is suitable for regular savings. Ideally designed for five years, the capital could be withdrawn earlier but you would have to sacrifice the tax-free bonus on the interest earned. If you have to dip into your Tessa for an emergency, then it becomes just like another building society account. If you are fortunate and emergencies don't strike, then your Tessa retains its tax-free benefits.

Financial protection for your family

If you die prematurely, your wife and children will need capital and/or income to replace your earnings. If you are unable to work through ill-health or disability they will need capital and/or income to replace your savings.

Most of your savings and investments will form part of your estate and be tied up until probate (if you have made a will) or letters of administration (if you have not) has been granted.

Even more to the point, are your savings and investments sufficient to provide adequate financial protection for your dependants?

Life insurance policies, written in trust for the benefit of a man's wife (or wife's husband) and/or his (her) children, will, on the death of the policyholder, immediately pay out the proceeds, the sum assured plus any bonuses which might have been added, without waiting for either a grant of probate or letters of administration.

The sum assured is likely to be considerably larger than your savings, particularly if you are a younger person. One guideline is that your life insurance cover should be up to five times salary, including your endowment mortgage, mortgage protection policy and any death-in-service pension scheme benefits.

Permanent health insurance policies will pay an income for the rest of your working life should you be unable to work.

The life insurance contracts discussed in the second section of the book are basically to be considered as investments, as their life insurance element is minimal.

Saving for a house

Although it is sometimes possible to obtain a 100 per cent home loan, most people, wisely, prefer to save for a home. If mortgage funds are in short supply (which seems increasingly unlikely as new lenders enter the market), regular savings will also help secure your mortgage.

Consider:

Bank Monthly Savings Account, or Mortgage Savings Account, if available

Building Society Monthly Savings Account

Lump sum savings towards your own home should not be locked away for longer than one month.

Consider:

Building Society Instant Access Account

Building Society Notice Account

Bank High Interest Deposit Account
National Savings Bank Investment Account

Saving for retirement

Apart from the state flat pension, paid for from National Insurance Contributions, everyone should now be entitled to a second pension, through a company pension scheme, personal pension plan or state earnings related scheme (SERPS).

The question is whether your pension will be large enough in retirement. Many people began making their pension arrangements later in life and might not have made sufficient pension payments to look forward to a financially comfortable retirement.

With the help of your pension scheme manager, check the current day value of your future pension, and compare it with your current expenditure. If the shortfall between the two is too large today, it will almost certainly be too large when you reach retirement.

Employees augment your retirement pension by:

Pensions – Additional Voluntary Contributions – either to the company pension scheme, or to a "free-standing" AVC scheme of your own choice.

Self-employed augment your retirement pension by:

Pensions – further contribution to Self-Employed Retirement Annuity (taken out before 1 July 1988), or the Personal Pension Plan which succeeded it. Then carry forward contributions to top up premiums for earlier tax years.

If you want to save more than the maximum annual savings (expressed as a percentage of income) permitted to these schemes or don't wish to commit your savings irrevocably towards pensions, then consider:

Life Insurance – With-Profits Endowment Policy
Life Insurance – With-Profits Flexible Endowment Policy
Life Insurance – Unit-Linked Savings Plan
Shares – Personal Equity Plans
Shares – Unit Trust and Investment Trust Savings Plans

For lump sum investments to build up your future capital for retirement, consider:

Life Insurance – Investment Bonds
Offshore – Managed Currency Fund
Shares – Investment Trust and Unit Trust
Shares – Ordinary
Shares – Personal Equity Plans

CHAPTER EIGHT

Savings strategies

Short term savings

Cars, holidays and weddings are three important reasons why people save; and most people have a fairly clear idea of how much they wish to spend on each.

For holidays, *consider:*

- Bank High Interest Deposit Account
- Bank High Interest Cheque Account
- Building Society Instant Access Account
- National Savings Bank Investment Account
- Offshore High Interest Cheque Account
- Offshore Single Currency Fund – for spending money

For cars, *consider:*

- Bank Monthly Savings Account
- Building Society Monthly Savings Account
- Building Society Instant Access Account
- National Savings Bank Investment Account

For weddings, *consider:*

- Holidays list if wedding within the coming 12 months
- Cars list, if wedding is longer than 12 months away

There are inheritance tax exemptions for family gifts of money to the bride and groom, see Chapter Four.

School fees

If you plan to educate your child privately, the earlier you start saving towards your offspring's future school fees, the better. The Assisted Places Scheme cuts the burden of school fees for the less well off parents. (Phone Independent Schools Information Service – 071-630 8793 – for more details.)

Regular savings towards future school fees needed in five or more years, consider:

- Building Society SAYE
- Bank or Building Society
- Tax Exempt Special Savings Account
- National Savings Yearly Plan
- Shares – Personal Equity Plans

Savings towards school fees needed in 10 or more years, consider:

- Bank or Building Society
- Tax Exempt Special Savings Account
- Shares – Personal Equity Plans
- Shares – Unit Trust Monthly Savings Schemes
- Shares – Investment Trust Monthly Savings Scheme
- Life Insurance – With-Profits Flexible Policy

Lump sums for school fees, consider:

- Life Insurance – Growth Bond
- Life Insurance – Investment Bond
- Life Insurance – School Fees Educational Trust
- Shares – Unit Trusts, Investment Trusts
- Stock – Government Fixed Interest, Government Index-Linked

An accumulation and maintenance trust is suitable for larger lump sums donated for the purposes of school fees by someone other than the parent, such as grandparent or godparent. There are tax advantages, see Chapter Three. A solicitor or accountant will advise you on setting up a trust.

Divorce

Maintenance payments under a court order or enforceable separation deed made after 14 March 1988 are tax free in the hands of the recipient. Under agreements made before then, payments to a spouse above £1,720 count as taxable income; payments to a child are taxable, but the child has the single person's allowance of £3,445 to offset against it.

The payer will not be entitled to tax relief on payments made under post 14 March agreements, except up to a limit equal to the difference between the personal allowance and married couple's allowance, now £1,720.

If cash settlement is made, suitable investments to provide a regular income are:

Building Society Monthly Income Account

National Savings Income Bond

Shares – Unit Trust Monthly Income Scheme

Divorce invalidates wills, widow's or widower's pension rights (unless a judge orders otherwise) and affects life insurance policies where the proceeds are in trust for a wife/husband. Both parties should check their position.

Redundancy

Only the first £30,000 of a lump sum redundancy payment is tax free.

If you are over 50, you might be given retirement as well as redundancy and be entitled to a pension and cash commutation of your pension rights; this lump sum is also tax free.

Unemployment benefit, which lasts for one year, is taxable. If you are still unemployed, then you might qualify for income support, which is tax free, provided your savings do not exceed £3,000.

Whether you are planning to go into business on your own, or feel you might have to delve into your redundancy money for survival, the same rule applies: do not tie up your money for anything longer than one to three months, and be sure that you can get your money back in full. If you consider your unemployment as early retirement, look at the later sections in this chapter on retirement.

Lump sum investments

Bank High Interest Cheque Account

Bank High Interest Deposit Account

Building Society Instant Access Account

Building Society Notice Account

National Savings Bank Investment Account

Offshore High Interest Cheque Account

Widowhood

Widows get the widow's bereavement tax allowance of £1,720 both in the tax year of the husband's death, and the following tax year too. A widow with children will also get the additional personal allowance for children.

Widow's pensions and widowed mother's allowances are taxable; the child addition paid to the widow's benefit, if applicable, is tax free.

Any life insurance payable on her husband's death is tax free, even if it is paid in regular instalments as a family income benefit. A widow's pension from her husband's company pension scheme is taxable.

Some widows inherit substantial investment portfolios, and should take professional advice about them if they are inexperienced investors.

Non-working widows who are wanting monthly income should consider:

Building Society Monthly Income Account

National Savings Income Bond

and for future growth:

Shares – Unit Trust Monthly Income Plan

Retirement

The extra tax allowance for those over 65 and on modest incomes needs careful planning.

Anyone over 65 is entitled to the personal age allowance of £4,200. The married couple's allowance of £2,465 goes initially to the husband. If he is under 65 and his wife over 65, special arrangements are made to ensure that the couple are not worse off (in respect of their tax allowances) than they were in 1989–90.

When your income exceeds £14,200, the extra age allowance is reduced by £1 for every £2 of income until it is finally extinguished and you are on the normal tax allowance level. For the individual, this occurs when income reaches £15,710, for the person claiming the married couple's allowance it is £17,200.

There is an extra age allowance of £4,370 (personal) and £2,505 (married) for those over 75. The income limit remains £14,200; therefore the extra age allowance is reduced by £1 for every £2 of income until it is extinguished at £16,050 (personal), £17,620 (including married couple's allowance).

It is important to keep your income under the threshold of £14,200 if you are a borderline case, and look for income which does not have to be declared on your tax return.

Consider:

Bank or Building Society – Tax Exempt Special Savings Account

Life Assurance – Investment Bond 5 per cent withdrawal plan

National Savings Certificates – cashing units each year to provide an "income" and leaving your capital intact

Shares – Personal Equity Plan

Do not forget to gross up the interest paid by banks, building societies, deposit takers and local authorities in calculating your total income. If your total income is near the £14,200 level, the gross interest could result in some lost personal allowance. See Chapter Five.

Retirement can last a long time, and although more and more company pensions are increased in payment, it is not wise (if you have sufficient capital for a spread of investment) to have the rest of your retirement savings entirely in fixed capital investments. Interest rates can go down.

Consider:

Bank and Building Society – Tax Exempt Special Savings Account

Building Society Instant Access

Bank High Interest Cheque Account

Offshore High Interest Account

National Savings Income Bonds

Shares – Unit Trust – Monthly Income Plan

Shares – Investment Trusts

Very old

Annuities begin to look attractive for men and women in their seventies. Home income plans, a way of boosting retirement income by using the capital tied up in your own home, are available to individuals over 70, married couples with a joint age of 150 years.

CHAPTER NINE

Investor protection

There are two kinds of risk facing the investor.

Investment risk is the possibility of losing some, even all, of your money in an asset which fluctuates in value, see Chapter Two.

The other kind of risk investors take is that the body or institution looking after their money might go bust; or that the person or organisation handling your investments might go bust or fail to invest your money for you.

Various safeguards exist to protect investors from such eventualities, however unlikely they might be in some cases. And if the worst were to happen, compensation schemes will provide some financial consolation.

Financial Services Act

This major piece of investor protection legislation came into force in stages in 1988.

The Securities and Investments Board (SIB) has the power through satellite Self-Regulatory Organisations (SROs) to vet all investment businesses.

The SROs which most concern the private investor are:

Financial Intermediaries, Managers and Brokers Regulatory Association (FIMBRA) covers insurance brokers and other financial intermediaries giving independent financial advice.

Life Assurance and Unit Trust Regulatory Organisation (LAUTRO) covers organisations selling life insurance and unit trusts.

Investment Managers Regulatory Organisation (IMRO) covers all investment management organisations such as unit trust, investment trust, pension fund and life insurance fund management.

The Securities & Futures Authority (SFA) covers stockbrokers and securities dealers and now includes the Association of Futures Brokers and Dealers.

It is a criminal offence to carry on an investment business without authorisation from either SIB or the appropriate SRO.

SIB holds a complete list of authorised firms or individuals. Make sure that your investment adviser, fund manager or stockbroker is authorised by calling 071-929 3652. You will be told the firm's full name, head office address, which SRO it is authorised by and the areas of business the firm is authorised to deal in.

Each SRO has established a complaints procedure to assist investors with a grievance. In addition each has appointed an ombudsman or referee to deal impartially with investors' complaints which the normal procedure has not resolved. The ombudsmen have the power to make financial awards in the case of maladministration etc. They do not investigate a disappointing investment performance.

The telephone numbers for the four SROs with which you are likely to have the most contact are:

FIMBRA:	071-538 8860
LAUTRO:	071-379 0444
IMRO:	071-379 0601
SFA:	071-256 9000

In the event of an authorised investment business failing, the Financial Services Act provides some measure of compensation.

SIB Compensation Scheme covers 100 per cent of the first £30,000 of savings and 90 per cent of the next £20,000, an overall maximum compensation of £48,000.

Individual SROs' compensation schemes mirror SIB's.

There are other compensation schemes available to investors. These are:

Banks and deposit takers are both classified as "authorised institutions" by the Bank of England. The level of compensation is up to 75 per cent of the first £20,000 of deposits.

Banking activity which needs authorisation under the Financial Services Act is covered by the compensation scheme of the appropriate SRO.

The Banking Ombudsman (tel: 071-583 1395) will investigate complaints that normal banking complaints procedures fail to solve.

Building societies are exempt from the SIB or SROs' compensation scheme, but societies' own statutory compensation scheme covers 90 per cent of savings up to £20,000.

The Building Societies Ombudsman (tel: 071-931 0044) will deal with intractable complaints.

UK authorised insurance companies are covered by the Policyholders Protection Act providing 90 per cent of policy benefits, provided these are not "excessive". This compensation scheme remains in force. The Insurance Ombudsman (tel: 071-928 7600) has limited powers to investigate life assurance contracts in the case of an intractable dispute.

Unit trusts no longer have their own individual Ombudsman, but come under the wing of the Insurance Ombudsman (tel: 071-928 7600).

National Savings are guaranteed by the Government.

Savings and Investments

BANK

Cash Card Account

Cash card accounts offer an easy withdrawal and deposit system through the hole-in-the-wall cash machines and other cash dispensers or automated teller machines (ATMs). They usually pay higher rates of interest than interest bearing current accounts. Other services are often included such as standing orders and mini statements.

Suitable for: Salary transfers, day-to-day money management for cash, rather than cheque book oriented customers. Older children who do not need or want a cheque book facility.

Open to: Anyone usually over 16.

Min–Max: £1; no maximum.

Charges: None.

Withdrawals: Up to £100–£250 a day cash from ATMs.

Interest: Variable; usually paid half-yearly or annually. Rates are tiered so that the more you have, the more you earn.

Tax: Interest is added net of basic rate tax; higher rate taxpayers must pay more. Banks can pay interest gross to non-taxpayers; non-taxpayers who fail to register will still be able to reclaim the basic rate tax deducted at source.

Children: Yes.

How to invest: At your local branch including Barclays, National Westminster and Yorkshire.

Record: Regular statements.

Money Mail Rating: *****

Investor protection: Bank savings compensation scheme covers 75 per cent of savings up to £20,000, maximum payout £15,000 per person.

Comment: Compare facilities and rates with accounts offered by building societies. Lloyds account is aimed at higher end of market and makes a monthly charge if the balance falls below £1,000. National Westminster's First Reserve, aimed at first time savers, offers competitive rates of interest for low level of savings.

Children's Account

Bank accounts offering children a range of free gifts and magazines. Some banks now have a separate account for older children and young people with a cash dispenser card. Midland, TSB and Yorkshire are the most active banks on the school banking scene.

Suitable for: Children's pocket money and encouraging money management.

Open to: Children up to 16, occasionally 14. Afterwards account reverts to deposit or cash card account.

Min–Max: Ranges from £1–£10; no maximum.

Withdrawals: Either seven days' notice (or loss of seven days' interest if immediate) or immediate withdrawal. Instant cash dispenser withdrawals allowed in most cases for young people over 13 years.

Interest: Variable; usually paid half-yearly into account, banks can pay interest gross to non-taxpayers.

Children: Yes, but parent's signature required for withdrawals for under sevens.

How to invest: Apply at bank branch. Obtain form to register child as non-taxpayer from branch. Only parents can sign on behalf of a child.

Record: Half-yearly statements and paying-in books.

Money Mail Rating: *****

Investor protection: Bank savings compensation scheme covers 75 per cent of savings up to £20,000. Maximum payout £15,000 per person.

Comment: Convenience, including a Saturday morning branch (as banking hours do not fit in with school hours), and highest available interest rate should be just as important as the free gifts, money boxes and magazines!

Check whether local building societies' children's schemes offer a higher rate of interest; the gifts will be less impressive. For larger sums, consider money which can be "locked up", possibly with a higher interest rate.

Deposit Account

Basic bank interest-bearing account requiring seven days' notice to withdraw funds or loss of seven days' interest if withdrawn immediately. No cheque book.

Suitable for: Lump sums below the threshold for High Interest Deposit Account, but not recommended.

Open to: Anyone.

Min–Max: £1 minimum; no maximum.

Withdrawals: Any amount at seven days' notice, or immediately with loss of seven days' interest.

Interest: Variable, usually paid half-yearly either to this account or current account.

Tax: Interest is paid net of tax; higher rate taxpayers pay more. Banks can pay interest gross to non-taxpayers.

Children: Yes, but Bank Children's Account a better investment.

How to invest: At any branch of most banks. You need not have a current account with the bank. Register at branch to obtain gross interest.

Record: Usually none. Half-yearly statement. Keep paying-in slip stubs.

Money Mail Rating: *****

Investor protection: Bank savings compensation scheme covers 75 per cent of savings up to £20,000.

BANK

Comment: It is hard to make a case for investing in a Bank Deposit Account which pays the lowest rate of interest of all bank accounts, and less than building society ordinary account. Non-taxpayers consider National Savings Investment Account.

High Interest Cheque Account

Interest bearing current account, usually with minimum starting investment often £2,000–£2,500. It is a cheque book account, but some banks stipulate minimum cheque withdrawal of £200–£250. Standing orders and overdrafts are allowed; sometimes run primarily in conjunction with group's investment management arm. Credit card facility often included.

Suitable for: Investors with frequent high value transactions such as school fees and large household bills; bank customers who habitually keep too much in their current account or keep household running funds in interest bearing but less flexible building society account.

Open to: Anyone aged 18 or over.

Min–Max: Minimum commonly £2,000–£2,500, but can be as low as £500. No maximum.

Charges: In most cases none. If balance with Save & Prosper account drops below set level £5 a month; limited number of free cheques at some banks.

Withdrawals: Sometimes minimum cheque withdrawal of £200–£250, but most groups have no minimum cheque withdrawals. Where a credit card is part of the package, monthly repayment can be below minimum cheque level.

Interest: Variable, calculated daily; sometimes tiered rate so larger amounts earn more. Make sure you keep the minimum opening balance in the account or you will get a very low interest rate.

Tax: Interest is paid net of tax; higher rate taxpayers pay more. Banks can pay interest gross to non-taxpayers; non-taxpayers who fail to register as such will still be able to reclaim the basic rate tax deducted at source.

Children: Not unless account held in adult's name.

How to invest: Apply in writing or through branch network to Abbey National, Allied Trust Bank, Bank of Ireland, Bank of Scotland, Barclays, Caledonian Bank, Carter Allen, Clydesdale, Gartmore, Kleinwort Benson, Lloyds, Midland, National Westminster, Royal Bank of Scotland, Save & Prosper (Robert Fleming), Schroder, Tyndall, Western Trust.

Record: Bank statement, usually quarterly.

Money Mail Rating: *****

Investor protection: Bank savings compensation scheme covers 75 per cent of savings up to £20,000. Maximum payout £15,000 per person.

Comment: Without a cheque guarantee card, it is hard to see this account really overthrowing the bank current account, even when it is used extensively in conjunction with a credit card for retail purchases. But with full banking facilities – cheque guarantee card, standing order payments and overdrafts – it can replace the current account entirely.

---

* *Both are classified as "authorised institutions" under The Banking Act 1987.*

Instant Access Account

An easy access high interest bearing account, with a minimum balance of often at least £1,000, frequently with tiered interest rate structure so that larger amounts earn more. A monthly income facility is sometimes included.

Suitable for: Lump sum investments for emergencies, day-to-day money management, irregular savings, "rainy day" money.

Open to: Anyone.

Min–Max: £500–£2,000 minimum; no maximum.

Charges: None.

Withdrawals: On demand from any branch.

Interest: Variable, usually tiered so that larger sums earn more, paid quarterly or annually. Rates usually higher than High Interest Cheque Account.

Tax: Interest is paid net of tax; higher rate taxpayers pay more. Banks can pay interest gross to non-taxpayers; non-taxpayers who fail to fill in the self-certification form will still be able to reclaim the basic rate tax deducted at source.

Children: Yes, but parent's signature for withdrawals for under sevens.

How to invest: At branch or apply in writing to Abbey National, Allied Trust, Barclays, Clydesdale, Co-operative Bank, First Direct, Gartmore, Girobank, Lloyds, Midland, National Westminster, Royal Bank of Scotland, TSB, Tyndall.

Record: Bank statement.

Money Mail Rating: *****

Investor protection: Bank savings compensation scheme covers 75 per cent of savings up to £20,000. Maximum payout £15,000 per person.

Comment: Much better than ordinary deposit account; always compare rates with building society instant access accounts. National Westminster First Reserve, aimed at first time savers, has minimum opening balance of just £1 and gives a cash card.

Interest-Bearing Current Account

In the wake of increased competition from building societies, most of the High Street banks have launched one or more current accounts which pay interest. Such an account should not be viewed as an investment.

Suitable for: Day-to-day money management for people who habitually keep their current accounts in credit.

Open to: Anyone over 18.

Min–Max: £1; no maximum.

Charges: Free if account in credit. Often a monthly or quarterly fee for overdrawn customers.

Withdrawals: On demand.

Interest: Variable, and often tiered so large balances earn more.

Tax: Interest is paid net of tax; higher rate taxpayers will pay more. Banks can pay interest gross to non-taxpayers; non-taxpayers who fail to register will still be able to reclaim the basic rate tax deducted at source.

Children: No, if automatic loan facilities are included in the account package. Children's savings accounts can be converted later.

How to invest: At any branch of most banks.

Record: Regular statements.

Money Mail Rating: *****

Investor protection: Bank compensation scheme covers 75 per cent of credit balances up to £20,000, maximum payout £15,000 per person.

Comment: Rates vary, so choose bank with best rate for your likely balance. Charges can be high if overdrawn over a certain limit, usually £100–£250, so accounts more suitable for individuals who retain a credit balance each month rather than going into the red.

Monthly Income Account

Lump sum investment, which can usually be increased at any time, which pays higher rate interest monthly into the customer's current account. Withdrawal notice period varies from none to one year according to account to which the facility is linked.

Suitable for: Those needing to boost monthly income who have a current or other account for day-to-day money management.

Open to: Anyone.

Min–Max: £1,000–£2,500 minimum; no maximum.

Charges: None.

Withdrawals: Withdrawals after notice period if any.

Interest: Variable, paid monthly. Rates tiered so that the more you invest, the more you earn; rates substantially better for those with £10,000 or more. Abbey National, Allied Trust and First Direct normally pay competitive rates.

Tax: Interest is paid net of tax; higher rate taxpayers pay more. Banks can pay interest gross to non-taxpayers; non-taxpayers who fail to register will still be able to reclaim the basic rate tax deducted at source.

Children: Not suitable.

How to invest: At any branch of most banks.

Record: Regular statements.

Money Mail Rating: *****

Investor protection: Bank savings compensation scheme covers 75 per cent of savings up to £20,000, maximum payout £15,000 per person.

Comment: Always compare rate with building society monthly income accounts and National Savings Income Bond.

Monthly Savings Account

Regular monthly savings scheme for unlimited period. Your level of savings can be varied after six months and you can miss one month's savings without penalty. If savings cease account reverts to deposit account.

Suitable for: Regular savings of small amounts; short term savings such as for a holiday or specific purchase; first time savers.

Open to: Anyone.

Min–Max: £10 a month minimum; usually no maximum.

Charges: None.

Withdrawals: Withdrawal usually permitted once every six months.

Interest: Variable; paid half-yearly in most cases either to this account or current account.

Tax: Interest is paid net of tax; higher rate taxpayers pay more. Banks can pay interest gross to non-taxpayers; non-taxpayers who fail to register will still be able to reclaim the basic rate tax deducted at source.

Children: Yes; investments in a child's name cannot be withdrawn by under sevens.

How to invest: Apply at branch of any bank; you need not have a current account with the bank.

Record: Half-yearly or annual statements.

Money Mail Rating: *****

Investor protection: Bank savings compensation scheme covers 75 per cent of savings up to £20,000, maximum payout £15,000 per person.

Comment: There are small interest rate variations on this account at different banks. Girobank pays a competitive rate. Compare with bank and building society instant access accounts with low minimum opening balance of £1 such as National Westminster First Reserve and Nationwide Cashbuilder.

Notice Account

Lump sum investment which requires notice of one, two, three or six months to withdraw funds. Investors have the option of losing interest for relevant period and instant access on funds.

Suitable for: Relatively short term "parking" of money not immediately required nor considered as part of your emergency money.

Open to: Anyone.

Min–Max: £100–£500 minimum. £25,000–£50,000 maximum.

Charges: None.

Withdrawals: Partial or full withdrawals permitted after specified notice period or loss of interest if you accept loss of interest for notice period. If you keep a balance, usually of £10,000, instant withdrawal from the surplus usually allowed without penalty. National Westminster allows £250 a month withdrawal without penalty.

Interest: Variable, usually paid half-yearly or quarterly. It can be paid by cheque, or direct into a bank account, or reinvested.

Tax: Interest is paid net of tax; higher rate taxpayers pay more. Banks can pay interest gross to non-taxpayers; non-taxpayers who fail to register will still be able to reclaim the basic rate tax deducted at source.

Children: Yes, parent's signature normally required for under sevens.

How to invest: Check interest rates at local branch.

Investor protection: Bank savings compensation scheme covers 75 per cent of savings up to £20,000, maximum payout £15,000 per person.

Comment: In general bank savings rates have become much more competitive in recent years. Compare interest rates and investment minimum with building society instant access accounts. Abbey National and National Westminster offer good 90 days' notice accounts, TSB 60 days' notice, Barclays one month's notice.

Save As You Earn (SAYE)

2nd Issue

Regular monthly savings scheme for five years with option to leave investment for further two years. Interest, which accumulates, is tax free and in addition there is a bonus equivalent to 14 months' payments, tax free, at the end of five years, or 28 months' if you leave the savings in for the next two years. A gap of six months' savings can be made up.

Suitable for: Higher rate taxpayers, regular savings for unspecified purpose, particularly when interest rates are falling.

Open to: Anyone aged 16 or over who does not have a SAYE account elsewhere.

Min–Max: £1 a month minimum; £20 maximum.

Charges: None.

Withdrawals: No partial withdrawals; repayment takes two to three weeks. Reduced interest rate penalties on early withdrawals: no interest in year one, years two to five interest of 6 per cent only (8 per cent if you die).

Interest: Fixed. Including the bonus, the rate is equivalent to 8.3 per cent a year over five years; including the enlarged bonus, the rate over seven years is equivalent to 8.62 per cent a year. It accumulates and is paid out when contract matures.

Tax: Tax free.

Children: No.

How to invest: Apply at bank branches.

Record: Certificate.

Money Mail Rating: *****

Investor protection: Bank savings compensation scheme covers 75 per cent of savings up to £20,000.

Comment: All banks will offer identical terms, so convenience is the main yardstick. Be sure you can keep up the savings for five years; early surrender rates unattractive.

Save As You Earn (SAYE)

Series "D" Share Option Scheme

Regular monthly savings linked to a company share option scheme. Employees are offered the option to buy shares at a price fixed at the start of the five year savings period which cannot be less than 80 per cent of market value. Employees invest a set amount each month in the SAYE scheme. At the end of five years they can either use the money to exercise the share option or take the money. They can leave the money invested for another two years to obtain the higher bonus BUT they will then lose the share option entitlement. However, some employers offer a seven year share option plan when the share option can then be exercised.

Interest in the SAYE accumulates tax free. In addition there is a bonus of 15 months' payments tax free at the end of five years, or 30 months' if you leave the savings in for the next two years. From 1 October these bonus levels reduce to 12.5 times the monthly contribution and 25 times respectively.

Suitable for: Employees who want to build up a share stake in their company.

Open to: Employers running a scheme fix the eligibility rules, usually determined by length of service with the company. Employees may have more than one share option SAYE scheme, provided the overall monthly contribution does not exceed the maximum.

Min–Max: £10 a month minimum; £250 maximum.

Charges: None.

Withdrawals: No partial withdrawals. Reduced interest rate penalties on early withdrawal; no interest in year one, years two to five, 5 per cent only. If you die, your executor can either take the amount saved or buy shares at the option price.

Interest: Fixed. Including the bonus is equivalent to 8.86 per cent over five years; including the enlarged bonus, the rate over seven years is equivalent to 9.15 per cent. It is accumulated. From 1 October the returns reduce to 7.5 per cent and 7.83 per cent.

Tax: Tax free. Once the share option is exercised, dividends are taxable and there is a potential gains tax liability, based on the actual purchase price of the shares, when you sell them.

Children: No.

How to invest: You will be invited to participate by your employer who must have Inland Revenue approval for the scheme.

Record: Certificate.

Money Mail Rating: ***** until the share option is exercised.

Investor protection: Bank compensation scheme covers 75 per cent of savings up to £20,000, maximum payout £15,000 per person.

Comment: A useful way of hedging your bets. If the company's share rise has risen since you were granted the option, then you exercise the option and buy the share at lower price fixed when you began savings. You will have a built-in profit. However, if your company has been less successful and the share price is actually lower than the option price, then take the SAYE proceeds as cash.

Tax Exempt Special Savings Account

Tessa, for short, is a new form of saving available since the beginning of 1991. It is a five year account for either regular or irregular lump savings and provided the capital is left intact for five years, the interest is tax free. If the interest is withdrawn before then, it will be paid net of basic rate tax, but the amount reserved for tax will be paid as tax-free bonus at the end of the five year period. If the capital is withdrawn before, the interest is taxable.

Suitable for: Erratic lump sum savers, taxpayers and "rainy day" savings.

Open to: Anyone over 18.

Min–Max: Overall maximum over five years, £9,000. Maximum per month £150. Maximum lump £3,000 in year one, £1,800 in years two to four, £600 in year five.

Charges: None.

Withdrawals: Interest can be taken net within the five year period. Capital at any time, but tax advantages will be lost.

Interest: Variable, usually annual. Confederation Bank offers fixed rate scheme.

Tax: Interest is tax free provided capital not withdrawn early. If net interest is taken during the five year span, the amount reserved for tax will be paid as a tax-free bonus at the end of the term.

Children: No.

Record: Initial certificate and annual update.

Money Mail Rating: *****

Comment: An attractive and flexible savings vehicle, suitable for second line emergency savings. Tessas may be transferred from one deposit taker to another but this may entail a loss of bonus or a charge. Not all providers allow transfers into their schemes. Compare with rates offered by building societies. Pick a plan with attractive rates but with no penalties on transfer out. Abbey National offers competitive plan but does not, as yet, allow transfers in.

Term Account

Lump sum, fixed interest rate investment with money tied up for one month to five years. The interest rate does not necessarily vary with the length of the investment. Variable rate schemes also available.

BANK AND DEPOSIT TAKER

Suitable for: Anyone taking a view that interest rates elsewhere will fall soon and wants to lock into fixed rates.

Open to: Anyone.

Min–Max: Minimum commonly £2,000, but can be as little as £500 or as much as £5,000. Usually no maximum.

Charges: None.

Withdrawals: At end of term, other than in exceptional circumstances, but interest rate usually reduced.

Interest: Fixed, higher rates sometimes negotiable for larger sums. Although fixed for the term, the rates quoted for new deposits change in line with other bank interest rates. For shorter term investments interest payable at maturity, otherwise half-yearly or annually.

Tax: Interest is paid net of tax; higher rate taxpayers pay more. Banks can pay interest gross to non-taxpayers; non-taxpayers who fail to register will still be able to reclaim the basic rate tax deducted at source.

Children: Not suitable.

How to invest: Interest rates quoted in bank branches and newspaper advertisements (deposit takers). Apply at branch, or in writing.

Record: Statement.

Money Mail Rating: *****

Investor protection: Bank savings compensation scheme covers 75 per cent of savings up to £20,000.

Comment: Locking up your money at a fixed rate of interest for a long period is usually inadvisable because of the loss of flexibility. But when interest rates are exceptionally high they could be a bargain. Compare returns with guaranteed income bonds over the same investment time span. Abbey National offers variable rate term shares.

Cash Card Account

Cash card accounts, operating through LINK network, offer an easy withdrawal and deposit system through the hole-in-the-wall cash machines and other cash dispensers or automated teller machines (ATMs). Other services too in some cases such as standing orders and mini statements are available. Originally introduced as an alternative to a cheque book account, in practice more and more societies are adding cheque book facilities.

Suitable for: Salary transfers. Day-to-day money management for cash, rather than cheque book oriented customers. Older children, particularly the technology minded.

Open to: Anyone over age 13, sometimes 16.

Min–Max: £1 minimum; no maximum.

Charges: None.

Withdrawals: Up to £100–£250 a day cash from ATMs; larger cheque withdrawals at counter.

Interest: Variable. Account can be tied into either ordinary or instant access accounts and those interest rates and tiers, if relevant, apply. Interest usually paid half-yearly or annually and accumulated.

Tax: Interest is paid net of tax; higher rate taxpayers must pay more. Building societies can pay interest gross to non-taxpayers; non-taxpayers who fail to register will still be able to reclaim the basic rate tax deducted at source.

Children: Yes, over age 13–16.

How to invest: At local branch. Larger societies offering this account include Alliance & Leicester, Birmingham Midshires, Bradford & Bingley, Bristol & West, Derbyshire, Halifax.

Record: Passbook if tied to other account, otherwise regular statements (which can be updated at the ATM).

Money Mail Rating: *****

Investor protection: Building society savings compensation scheme covers 90 per cent of savings up to £20,000, maximum payout £15,000 per depositor.

Comment: Building societies have pushed this account hard as an alternative to much more expensive to administer (from their point of view) cheque book facilities, but are increasingly offering both. Direct debiting from the card account in stores is a development to watch. Alliance & Leicester offers telephone banking service through its "Cash Plus" account.

Cheque Book Account

Several large societies offer a full cheque book banking service, including a cheque guarantee card, complete with current account interest. Other societies run cheque book accounts but not with full banking facilities (see High

Interest Cheque Accounts). Some of the existing cheque book accounts neither permit overdrafts nor have a cheque guarantee card, but do usually have a credit card link.

Suitable for: Is becoming increasingly competitive with a bank current account and charges tend to be lower.

Open to: Anyone aged 18 or over.

Min–Max: Varies from £1 upwards minimum up to £100,000 maximum.

Charges: Cheques usually free unless account drops below minimum balance, if required. Charges for bounced or stopped cheques. Overdraft interest.

Withdrawals: By cheque, cash on demand up to £250, cash withdrawal machine.

Interest: Variable, and sometimes tiered so that the more you have in your account, the more you earn. Interest usually paid yearly. Northern Rock pay monthly.

Tax: Interest is paid net of tax; higher rate taxpayers pay more. Building societies can pay interest gross to non-taxpayers; non-taxpayers who fail to register will still be able to reclaim the basic rate tax deducted at source.

How to invest: At branches of Britannia, Chelsea, Halifax, Nationwide, Northern Rock, North of England, Norwich & Peterborough and Woolwich.

Record: Passbook and cheque book stub for additional reference or a monthly bank statement and no passbook.

Money Mail Rating: *****

Investor protection: Building society compensation scheme covers 90 per cent of savings up to £20,000, maximum payout £18,000 per person.

Comment: Accounts need to be run in conjunction with a credit card to be really effective. Accounts are fully competitive and should be compared with bank interest bearing current accounts. Which suits you best depends on how you run your financial affairs. Among the building societies Britannia, Chelsea and Northern Rock usually offer good rates.

Children's Account

Incentive account to attract young people into becoming savers with the help of favourite cartoon characters, gifts, comics, badges, pens and money boxes. Most societies pay their junior members more than ordinary account rate. There are different accounts for different ages, generally up to 11, and 11 and over.

Suitable for: Pocket money and lump sums and teaching children how to manage their own savings.

Open to: Children up to a stipulated age, most commonly 16 or 18 but sometimes as low as 10. A handful of societies have lower age limit of five.

Min–Max: £1 minimum; no maximum.

Charges: None.

Withdrawals: On demand from any

branch up to £250 cash, cheques up to £5,000. Parent's signature required for withdrawals under the age of seven, occasionally until child reaches age 10 or 12.

Interest: Variable with wide variations in rates. Some pay a narrow margin over the miserly ordinary share rate while others are much more generous. Interest paid annually or half-yearly and accumulates.

Tax: Building societies can pay interest gross to non-taxpayers, including children. Children must be registered as non-taxpayers by their parents. Forms available in branches.

How to invest: Over 40 societies, including all the major ones, run Children's Accounts. Apply at local branch.

Record: Passbook. Britannia runs a cash card account for 11 plus.

Money Mail Rating: *****

Investor protection: Building society compensation scheme covers 90 per cent of savings up to £20,000, maximum payout £18,000 per person.

Comment: Convenience for school or Saturday leisure activities is the most important aspect of a children's account, and in this respect the building society still scores over the children's bank account which is inaccessible on weekdays during term time. Money-wise kids will appreciate higher interest rates more than the "freebies". Parents should watch the tax trap if money they give to their offspring is invested in a children's account. Tax-free National Savings Certificates or Children's Bonus Bonds would be more appropriate for their regular or substantial money gifts.

Britannia offers attractive account with good rates of interest (with card and passbook) for those aged 11–15. Melton Mowbray's Sunny Bond has earned a reputation for good rates for the serious saver (£250 minimum).

Instant Access Account

Building society premium account offering high rates of interest, often on a tiered basis so that the more you invest, the more you earn. A monthly income facility is sometimes included. See also Postal Accounts.

Suitable for: Lump sum investments, particularly emergency funds; irregular savings; salary transfers and day-to-day money management.

Open to: Anyone.

Min–Max: £500–£1,000, occasionally as little as £1. No maximum.

Charges: None.

Withdrawals: On demand from any branch, usually up to £250 in cash, £5,000–£15,000 by cheque.

Interest: Variable. Rates are tiered so higher balances earn more. Large sums earn 1¼–1¾ per cent more than smaller amounts. If balance drops below minimum level then ordinary share rate payable. Interest usually paid annually to be accumulated or paid by cheque or direct into bank or other building society account. Monthly income sometimes available and may be at a slightly lower rate of interest.

Tax: Interest is paid net of tax; higher rate taxpayers pay more. Building societies can pay interest gross to non-taxpayers; non-taxpayers who fail to register will still be able to reclaim the basic rate of tax deducted at source.

Children: Yes, but parent's signature required for under sevens.

How to invest: Apply at branch or agency. Postal service frequently available.

Record: Passbook.

Money Mail Rating: *****

Investor protection: Building society savings compensation scheme covers 90 per cent of savings up to £20,000, maximum payout £18,000 per person.

Comment: A flexible and versatile account which permits easy switching of funds for those very interested in rates. Check carefully where the trigger points for the higher interest payments come: the first can be as high as £5,000 instead of the more common, and more easily attainable, £2,500. Interest paid half-yearly has a higher compound annual rate if you reinvest the interest. For smaller savers Portman (minimum £500) pays good rates. Alliance & Leicester and Woolwich also usually competitive.

High Interest Cheque Account

Interest bearing current account, with a minimum starting sum of £2,000 or £2,500, offered by a handful of societies. Account holders get a cheque book and usually a cash card, cheque guarantee card but no overdraft facility. Standing orders and direct debit facilities usually available. The interest rate drops dramatically if your balance falls below the usual minimum.

Suitable for: Investors with frequent high value transactions such as school fees and large household bills.

Open to: Anyone aged 18 or over.

Min–Max: commonly £2,000–£2,500.

Charges: None.

Withdrawals: By cheque or hole-in-the-wall machines with the cash card. Halifax stipulates a minimum cheque withdrawal of £200 and does not offer a cash card.

Interest: Variable and added monthly, quarterly or annually depending on the account. The rates are usually tiered so that the more you have in your account, the more you earn. Expect a derisory rate if your balance falls below the minimum opening balance.

Tax: Interest paid net of basic rate tax; higher rate taxpayers pay more. Building societies can pay interest gross to non-taxpayers. Non-taxpayers who fail to register will still be able to reclaim the basic rate tax deducted at source.

Children: No.

How to invest: Apply to High Street branches. Large building societies offering this type of account include Bristol & West, Chelsea, Halifax and Portman.

Record: Statement, usually quarterly.

Money Mail Rating: *****

Investor protection: Building society savings compensation scheme covers 90 per cent of savings up to £20,000, maximum payout £18,000 per person.

Comment: Compare with current accounts on offer from banks and make sure the account is flexible enough to meet your needs. Chelsea runs its Classic Account through the post. Halifax Asset Reserve Account, where interest rates are linked to the wholesale money market rates, has a higher than usual minimum balance of £5,000 and a minimum cheque withdrawal of £200.

Monthly Income Account

Lump sum investment which pays interest monthly and usually linked to either an instant access, notice account or term account, see page 50 and opposite. Some societies pay the same rates of interest in which case the compound annual rate (CAR) is higher; others trim the interest marginally because it is paid monthly.

Suitable for: Retired persons (but check the age allowance trap, see page 34) and others, such as non-working mothers, who need monthly income.

Open to: Anyone.

Min–Max: £2,000–£2,500 although occasionally lower. No maximum.

Charges: None.

Withdrawals: Same as for underlying account.

Interest: Variable, paid monthly either by cheque or direct to bank or other building society account. Halifax offers a fixed rate for one year.

Tax: Interest paid net of tax; higher rate taxpayers pay more. Gross interest available for registered non-taxpayers.

Children: Not suitable.

How to invest: Most societies have monthly income accounts. Apply at branch. Postal service frequently available.

Record: Passbook; half-yearly or annual statements as well in some cases.

Money Mail Rating: *****

Investor protection: Building society savings compensation scheme covers 90 per cent of savings up to £20,000, maximum payout £18,000 per person.

Comment: Shop around: interest rates and thresholds for higher interest rates on tiered accounts vary. Check the compound annual rate (CAR), particularly if you plan to reinvest rather than spend the income. Compare with National Savings Income Bonds and Guaranteed Income Bonds. Top rates from building societies usually available on term shares but instant access postal accounts run by Bradford & Bingley and Cheltenham & Gloucester offer good rates.

Notice Account

Lump sum investment account which requires notice of seven days, one, two or three months to withdraw funds. With accounts needing notice of one month or more, investors have the option of loss of interest for relevant period and instant access. Accounts are usually tiered so that the more you have invested, the more you earn. Monthly income usually available.

Suitable for: Lump sum investments needed at specific future date and longer term investments.

Open to: Anyone.

Min–Max: £500–£1,000 minimum; no maximum.

Charges: None.

Withdrawals: Any amount after required notice period, or instant access if you accept loss of interest for relevant notice period. This option not always available on seven day notice accounts. If you keep a balance usually of £10,000, instant withdrawal from surplus allowed.

Interest: Variable, usually paid annually to be accumulated or paid by cheque or direct into other account, or paid as monthly income. Larger investors earn 1.2–2 per cent more than smaller investors.

Tax: Interest is paid net of tax; higher rate taxpayers pay more. Gross interest available for registered non-taxpayers.

Children: Yes. Particularly for their long term savings. Parent's signature required for under sevens.

How to invest: Most societies have notice accounts. Apply at branch. Postal service frequently available.

Record: Passbook.

Money Mail Rating: *****

Investor protection: Building society savings compensation scheme covers 90 per cent of savings up to £20,000, maximum payout £18,000 per person.

Comment: Rates vary widely between societies and you can get up to 2 per cent more before tax by choosing the right society. Coventry, Skipton and Yorkshire are often among the best payers on 90 day accounts. Check the compound annual rate if interest paid monthly. When interest rates are fluctuating give your relevant notice immediately you make an investment in order to be able to switch funds quickly if a better interest rate opportunity appears.

Ordinary or Share Account

The basic no-strings, no-extras building society account offering easy access and miserly interest rates and should be avoided. Opt for instant access account with a low minimum balance instead. Deposit account, in return for 100 per cent security, has slightly lower interest rate.

Suitable for: It is hard to make a case for anyone. These accounts are very much the poor relation in the range.

Open to: Anyone.

Min–Max: £1. No maximum.

Charges: None generally but Halifax has introduced transaction charge for small savers.

Withdrawals: On demand from any branch or agency up to £250 in cash; by cheque from branches up to £5,000.

Interest: Variable; paid half-yearly to be accumulated or paid by cheque or direct into bank or other building society account.

Tax: Interest is paid net of tax; higher rate taxpayers pay more. Building societies can pay interest gross to non-taxpayers; non-taxpayers who fail to register will still be able to reclaim the basic rate of tax deducted at source.

Children: Yes, but parent's signature required for under sevens.

How to invest: At local branch or agency.

Record: Passbook.

Money Mail Rating: *****

Investor protection: Building society compensation scheme covers 90 per cent of savings up to £20,000, maximum payout £18,000 per person.

Comment: Increasingly obsolete account. Use Nationwide Cashbuilder account, an instant access with minimum opening balance of £1. Once you reach £100–£250 the choice gets wider with Leeds & Holbeck and National & Provincial. Children's Accounts frequently pay more to young savers irrespective of balance. Deposit accounts should be ignored.

Postal Account

A growing number of building societies operate accounts which are run exclusively through the post rather than the branch network. They offer attractive interest rates for those willing to operate the account using the first class post rather than a local branch. You can usually get your money back on demand but allow a couple of days for the post.

Suitable for: Anyone looking for good returns who is happy to run their account outside the High Street.

Open to: Anyone.

Min–Max: £1,000–£2,500; no maximum.

Charges: None.

Withdrawals: At any time on instructions sent via the post. The society provides paying-in and withdrawal slips.

Interest: Variable and tiered so that the more you have in your account, the more you earn. Interest is usually paid annually or monthly.

Tax: Interest is paid net of tax; higher rate taxpayers pay more. Building societies can pay interest gross to non-taxpayers; non-taxpayers who fail to register will still be able to reclaim the basic rate of tax deducted at source.

Children: Yes, parents operate the account.

How to invest: Through the post. Cheltenham & Gloucester allow you to open an account through their branch network, but thereafter it must be run through the post. Societies offering good paying postal accounts include Birmingham Midshires (90 day notice), Bradford & Bingley (instant access), Chelsea (with cheque book), Cheltenham & Gloucester (instant access) and Nationwide (term share). Other societies to watch which sometimes offer good accounts include Britannia, Leeds & Holbeck, Northern Rock, Norwich & Peterborough, Nottingham and Scarborough.

Record: Regular statements.

Money Mail Rating: *****

Investor protection: Building society compensation scheme covers 90 per cent of savings up to £20,000, maximum payout £18,000 per person.

Comment: Cheltenham & Gloucester has consistently paid good rates on its account, and Bradford & Bingley is determined to follow in its footsteps. Both accounts pay attractive annual and monthly rates: Bradford & Bingley rate is tiered starting at £1,000, while Cheltenham & Gloucester starts at £2,500 or £5,000 for monthly income. Bradford & Bingley allows you to run the account by post or telephone.

Regular Savings Account

Regular monthly savings scheme for unlimited period paying investors a higher rate of interest than on ordinary account. One withdrawal a year sometimes allowed, so is one month's savings lapse. It is usually possible to vary the amount saved.

Suitable for: Short-to-medium savings goals, such as a holiday, and more particularly a house.

Open to: Anyone.

Min–Max: £1–£10 a month minimum, £100–£250 maximum (doubled for joint accounts).

Charges: None.

Withdrawals: Partial withdrawals once or twice a year may be permitted, otherwise the account is closed or transferred to ordinary account.

Interest: Variable, paid half-yearly or annually and usually accumulated in the account. The rate is 1–1½ per cent above the ordinary rate.

Tax: Interest is paid net of tax; higher rate taxpayers pay more. Building societies can pay interest gross to non-taxpayers; non-taxpayers who fail to register will still be able to reclaim the basic rate of tax deducted at source.

Children: Not suitable.

How to invest: Most societies offer a regular savings scheme; apply at branch.

Record: Passbook.

Money Mail Rating: *****

Investor protection: Building society savings compensation scheme covers 90 per cent of savings up to £20,000, maximum payout £18,000 per person.

Comment: Interest rates on these accounts are not at the top of the building society range, so savers should use the account as a stepping stone to building up sufficient capital to transfer to higher paying instant access account.

Save As You Earn (SAYE)

2nd Issue

Regular monthly savings scheme for five years with option to leave investment for further two years. Interest, which accumulates, is tax free and in addition there is a bonus equivalent to 14 months' payments, tax free, at the end of five years, or 28 months' if you leave the savings in for the next two years. A gap of six months' savings can be made up.

Suitable for: Higher rate taxpayers, regular savings for unspecified purpose, particularly when interest rates are falling.

Open to: Anyone aged 16 or over.

Min–Max: £1 a month minimum; £20 maximum.

Charges: None.

Withdrawals: No partial withdrawals; repayment takes two to three weeks. Reduced interest rate penalties on early withdrawals: no interest in year one, years two to five interest of 6 per cent only (8 per cent if you die).

Interest: Fixed. Including the bonus, the rate is equivalent to 8.3 per cent a year over five years; including the enlarged bonus, the rate over seven years is equivalent to 8.62 per cent a year. It accumulates and is paid out when contract matures.

Tax: Tax free.

Children: No.

How to invest: Many societies operate a SAYE account but do not always promote it; apply at branch.

Record: Certificate.

Money Mail Rating: *****

Investor protection: Building society savings compensation scheme covers 90 per cent of savings up to £20,000, maximum payout £18,000 per person.

Comment: All societies offer identical terms, so convenience is the main yardstick. Be sure you can keep up the savings for five years; early surrender rates unattractive.

Save As You Earn (SAYE)

Series "D" Share Option Scheme

Regular monthly savings linked to a company share option scheme. Employees are offered the option to buy shares at a price fixed at the start of the five year savings period which cannot be less than 80 per cent of market value. Employees invest a set amount each month in the SAYE scheme. At the end of five years they can either use the money to exercise the share option or take the money; they can leave the money invested for another two years to obtain the higher bonus BUT they will then lose the share option entitlement. However, some employers offer a seven year share option plan when the share option can then be exercised.

Interest in the SAYE accumulates tax

free. In addition there is a bonus of 15 months' payments tax free at the end of five years, or 30 months' if you leave the savings in for the next two years. From 1 October the bonus levels reduce to 12.5 times the monthly contribution and 25 times respectively.

Suitable for: Employees who want to build up a share stake in their company.

Open to: Employers running a scheme fix the eligibility rules, usually determined by length of service with the company. Employees may have more than one share option SAYE scheme, provided the overall monthly contribution does not exceed the maximum.

Min–Max: £10 a month minimum; £250 a month maximum.

Charges: None.

Withdrawals: No partial withdrawals. Reduced interest rate penalties on early withdrawal; no interest in year one; years two to five, 5 per cent. If you die, your executor can either take the amount saved or buy shares at the option price.

Interest: Fixed. Including the bonus is equivalent to 8.86 per cent over five years; including the enlarged bonus, the rate over seven years is equivalent to 9.15 per cent. It is accumulated. From 1 October the returns will be 7.5 per cent and 7.83 per cent respectively.

Tax: Tax free. Once the share option is exercised, dividends are taxable and there is a potential gains tax liability, based on the actual purchase price of the shares, when you sell them.

Children: No.

How to invest: You will be invited to participate by your employer who must have Inland Revenue approval for the scheme.

Record: Certificate.

Money Mail Rating: ***** until the share option is exercised.

Investor protection: Building societies compensation scheme covers 90 per cent of savings up to £20,000, maximum payout £18,000 per person.

Comment: A useful way of hedging your bets. If the company's shares have risen since you were granted the option, then you exercise the option and buy the share at lower price fixed when you began savings. You will have a built-in profit. However, if your company has been less successful and the share price is actually lower than the option price, then take the SAYE proceeds as cash.

Tax Exempt Special Savings Account

Tessa, for short, is a new form of saving introduced at the beginning of 1991. It is a five year account for either regular or irregular lump savings and provided the capital is left intact for five years, the interest is tax free. If the interest is withdrawn before then, it will be paid net of basic rate tax, but the amount reserved for tax will be paid as tax-free bonus at the end of the five year period. If the capital is withdrawn before, the interest is taxable.

Suitable for: Erratic lump sum savers, taxpayers and "rainy day" savings.

Open to: Anyone over 18.

Min–Max: Overall maximum over five years, £9,000. Maximum per month £150. Maximum lump sum £3,000 in year one, £1,800 in years two to four, £600 in year five.

Charges: None.

Withdrawals: Interest can be taken net within the five year period. Capital at any time, but tax advantages will be lost.

Interest: Variable, usually annually.

Tax: Interest is tax free provided capital not withdrawn early. If net interest is taken during the five year span, the amount reserved for tax will be paid as a tax-free bonus at the end of the term.

Children: No.

Record: Initial certificate and annual update.

Money Mail Rating: *****

Comment: An attractive and flexible savings vehicle, suitable for second level emergency savings. Tessas may be transferred from one financial institution to another but this may entail a loss of bonus or a charge. Not all providers allow transfers into their scheme. Pick a plan with attractive rates and no transfer penalties. Britannia and Yorkshire are two large societies which have, to date, offered consistently competitive rates. Compare with plans on offer from banks and other deposit takers.

Term Share

Lump sum investment of declining popularity. Investors' funds are locked in for a period – the term – of one to five years, although withdrawals sometimes permitted with loss of interest penalty. Interest rate at the high end of the building society range, and often guaranteed differential over ordinary rate.

Suitable for: Modest lump sums which are too low to trigger off the top rates available on other accounts, provided the money is not going to be required.

Open to: Anyone.

Min–Max: £500–£1,000 minimum; no maximum.

Charges: None.

Withdrawals: Usually not allowed. Capital plus interest earned to date repaid on death within the term.

Interest: Usually variable, paid annually, half-yearly or monthly.

Tax: Interest is paid net of tax; higher rate taxpayers must pay more. Building societies can pay interest gross to non-taxpayers; non-taxpayers who fail to register will still be able to reclaim the basic rate of tax deducted at source.

Children: As tax paid, suitable for parents' gift of money. Higher rate tax parents will have to pay more. National Savings Certificates and Children's Bonus Bonds generally a better buy.

How to invest: Mainly offered by medium and smaller societies, and not always available. Apply at branches or by post and by newspaper advertisement.

Record: Passbook or certificate.

Money Mail Rating: *****

Investor protection: Building society savings compensation scheme covers 90 per cent of savings up to £20,000, maximum payout £18,000 per person.

Comment: Inflexible form of savings, and longer term periods should be avoided. Investors with larger sums will be able to obtain a higher interest on a more flexible instant access or notice account. Fixed interest term shares attractive when interest rates are falling. The guaranteed differential above the ordinary share rate can be less generous than it sounds as ordinary share rates tend to rise more slowly and fall further than other account rates.

MISSING MILLIONS

Unclaimed dividends, premium bond prizes and social security benefits run into millions of pounds. Unclaimed Premium Bond prizes (150,575 in all) alone total £9.76 million, and some £800 million of welfare benefits are not claimed, while the value of unclaimed dividends held in suspense accounts by publicly quoted companies can be counted in millions.

Does any of this money belong to you? The most common explanation is that people do not notify companies, Department of National Savings etc., when they change address. Share certificates can get overlooked when the shareholder dies.

Gold Coins

Gold coins are the easiest and most reliable way for a private investor to take a direct stake in gold. As a coin it is a non-income producing asset, it is held either purely for speculation that the price of gold, which can fluctuate considerably, will rise; or for the simple pleasure of owning it. The modern coins contain one Troy ounce of gold but stand at a premium to the price of gold, quoted in dollars per ounce. The EC banned the importation of South African Krugerrands in 1986. Other popular coins include the Canadian Maple Leaf and the Chinese Panda. The UK began minting a new gold coin, the Britannia, in 1987.

Suitable for: At the most 5 per cent to 10 per cent of savings and then only out of capital which will not be required at short notice. Alternative to cash gifts.

Open to: Anyone.

Min–Max: Current price of one gold coin – £198.25–£198.75, April 1992; – or less for Sovereigns which contain 0.2354 Troy oz gold – £47.25–£47.75, April 1992. No maximum.

Charges: Commission included in price of coin; 17.5 per cent VAT charged on all coins bought in the UK (except those more than 100 years old, where VAT is charged on the dealer's profit margins only). Coins bought, and held in Channel Islands or Gibraltar not subject to VAT, but a storage charge of typically £2 a coin and annual service fee of 50p per half-year, paid in arrears.

Withdrawals: At current market price, immediately.

Tax: Capital gains tax liability on profits except for pre-1838 Sovereigns.

Children: Gifts.

How to invest: Check prices, quoted in dollars, in newspaper. Most banks buy and sell gold coins but usually impose minimum of 10 coins/£3,000. Compare prices charged by dealers. A full coin dealing (and storage if required) service available from Braid & Co, Gold Investments Ltd, Spink & Son Ltd. If you deal through the Channel Islands and keep the coins there to avoid VAT, stick to subsidiaries of well-known UK banks.

Record: If you hold the coins yourself, none. If coins are held offshore, certificate and regular statement.

Money Mail Rating: *!!!! to !!!!!

Investor protection: Gold coins outside scope of Financial Services Act; in the UK store coins at bank; if coins kept in Channel Islands make sure coins are physically held in your name.

Comment: A limited exposure to gold can be very rewarding, particularly at time of international political uncertainty or strong currency fluctuations. However, it is worth noting that the gold price did not surge ahead in the Gulf War, as might have been expected. A platinum coin, the Isle of Man Noble, is also available, and in several denominations.

Annuity

Lump sum investment which cannot be redeemed, in return for which investors receive an income for life. The amount payable will depend upon your age: the older you are, the better the return. The interest paid is usually fixed at the outset. Annuity contracts can be varied to provide an income which continues until the surviving spouse dies, or a guaranteed income which continues for five or 10 years regardless of whether the annuitant survives.

Suitable for: Older men and women; fixed income offers little protection against rising costs in periods of high inflation.

Open to: Anyone, in theory, but rarely worthwhile for people under 70 (men) or 75 (women).

Min–Max: Minimum realistic level is around £1,000 – producing (at May 1992) £140–£145 p.a. income for men aged 70 and women 75. No maximum.

Charges: Built into the contract terms.

Withdrawals: None.

Interest: Fixed, according to each type of annuity. A few unit-linked contracts provide rising interest from a much lower starting base. Interest is usually paid in arrears by cheque or direct to a bank account monthly, quarterly, half-yearly or annually.

Tax: Part of the annuity is treated as return of capital and tax free, the remainder treated as income and has basic rate tax deducted at source. Non-taxpayers can be paid gross; higher rate taxpayers pay more.

Children: Not suitable.

How to invest: Most life insurance companies offer annuities. Check rates in specialist publications such as *Money Management* or *Planned Savings* and/or consult an insurance broker.

Record: Annuity contract, setting out the terms.

Money Mail Rating: *****

Investor protection: Policyholders protection scheme covers 90 per cent of benefits.

Comment: With modest inflation only, annuities can be worthwhile for the more elderly. Useful for inheritance tax planning for people with large estates. Older men and women owning their own property can release some of the capital "tied up" in the house with the use of Income Plan, based upon an annuity and mortgage package.

Guaranteed Income Bond and Guaranteed Growth Bonds

Lump sum investment with fixed return over term of one to five years commonly, sometimes six to 10 years and, rarely, sometimes as long as 15 years. If the bond pays out the interest, it is an Income Bond; if the income is accumu-

lated, it is Growth Bond. Underlying investments linked to fixed rate investments.

Suitable for: Augmenting retirement income (but check age allowance, see page 34); capital build up before retirement; specific savings target (Growth Bonds); taking a view on interest rates.

Open to: Minimum age often 16 or 18; maximum age commonly 80 or 85, occasionally 90.

Min–Max: Minimum £1,000–£2,000. Maximum none, or £50,000, £75,000 or £100,000.

Charges: Built into contract terms.

Withdrawals: At maturity, original investment – Income Bonds; guaranteed value – Growth Bonds; early surrender values, if available, usually poor. Death benefits: original investment – Income Bonds; original investment plus 6–9 per cent – Growth Bonds.

Interest: Fixed. Income Bonds pay monthly (the rate is usually marginally lower), half-yearly and most commonly annually. Interest accumulates with Growth Bonds.

Tax: Interest paid net of tax (Growth and Income Bonds alike) which usually cannot be reclaimed by non-taxpayers; higher rate taxpayers pay more.

Children: Not suitable.

How to invest: Some bonds only available for limited period, check newspapers for offers. Check rates in specialist publications such as *Money Management* or *Planned Savings* and/or consult an insurance broker. Stick to UK insurance companies.

Record: Insurance policy.

Money Mail Rating: *****

Investor protection: Policyholders protection scheme covers 90 per cent of benefits agreed by UK insurance companies, provided they are not excessive.

Comment: High fixed returns attractive if you think interest rates will fall. Insurance companies carefully "match" their underlying investments to provide the guaranteed return at a set date; but the guarantee is still only as good as the company issuing it, so always choose an authorised UK insurance company. Policies sold by an overseas life insurance company which is not authorised in the UK are not included in the policyholders protection scheme.

Investment Bond

Lump sum investment in single premium life insurance policy linked directly to an individual market sector, or mixture of different types of investment. There are investment bonds linked to UK equities, international equities, fixed interest stock, cash, convertible stock and property (Property Bond), both in the UK or overseas. Other bonds, known as Managed Bonds, are linked to a mixture of some or all of these investment categories. Investors can switch to one category from another in the same group without cashing in the policy.

Suitable for: Higher rate taxpayers and older people on modest incomes who are borderline cases in respect of the age allowance, see page 34, the extra tax relief given to some people over the age of 65.

Open to: Varies; anyone; from 14 or 18 minimum age to 80 maximum.

Min–Max: £500, commonly £1,000 and sometimes £2,500 minimum. No maximum.

Charges: Initial fee of 3–10 per cent deducted from initial investment; annual fee ½–¾ per cent.

Withdrawals: On demand, at current market value; on death current market value of units (more in earlier years).

Interest: Variable; accumulated within the fund. Up to 5 per cent of original investment can be withdrawn as "income" with income tax liability, applicable to higher rate taxpayers only, deferred until bond finally encashed, or after 20 years. "Income" withdrawal does not have to be declared on tax return.

Tax: Income tax and capital gains tax on realised gains paid by insurance company, reflected in the underlying unit price. Proceeds tax free for basic rate taxpayers; non-taxpayers cannot reclaim any income tax paid; higher rate taxpayers must pay more.

Children: Yes, where age limits permit.

How to invest: Check performance of underlying units in specialist publications such as *Money Management* or *Planned Savings*; phone or write for details from insurance companies before investing.

Record: Insurance policy.

Money Mail Rating: ****! to *!!!!

Investor protection: Policyholders protection scheme covers 90 per cent of current unit value.

Comment: Bond's internal capital gains tax liability major disadvantage compared with lump sum investment in unit trusts which roll up without capital gains tax. "Income" withdrawal beneficial to higher rate taxpayers who can defer tax liability until retirement when tax bracket likely to be lower; older people will not have their age allowance entitlement jeopardised by "income" withdrawal.

School Fees Educational Trust

Lump sum investment via a trust into a life insurance company for a child which will pay school fees on either a flat or increasing basis. It can be taken out immediately before the fees become due, or up to 13 years in advance. It is not essential to identify the school in advance, and you can change your mind and surrender the policy instead. Regular savings sometimes permitted if policy taken out at least three years ahead of first fee.

Suitable for: Parents, grandparents and any adult wishing to fund school fees in advance, particularly higher rate taxpayers.

Open to: Anyone.

Min–Max: Depends on the size of fees and the number of years ahead they are required. Minimum £500–£2,500; £50 a month; no maximum.

Charges: Built into the contract.

Withdrawals: Paid as agreed termly fees; if child dies 95–100 per cent of original purchase price plus interest; otherwise non-guaranteed surrender value.

Interest: Fixed; accumulated within the trust.

Tax: The fees from the trust are paid tax free as the person making the payment has no legal interest in the policy.

Children: Improbable – the trust is for their benefit.

How to invest: Equitable Life (which accepts monthly and irregular lump sum contributions), Royal Life, Save & Prosper, and School Fees Insurance Agency (SFIA) all have educational trust facilities.

Record: Contract with trust.

Money Mail Rating: *****

Investor protection: Policyholders protection scheme covers 90 per cent of benefits.

Comment: More flexible than investing school fees in advance via a "composition fee" scheme direct with the school of your choice. The earlier school fee investment is made, the smaller the capital outlay.

Unit-Linked Regular Savings Plan

Regular savings insurance policy for five, 10 years or indefinitely, linked directly to individual market sector, or mixture of different types of investment. Savings can be linked to specific unit trusts, UK equities, international equities, fixed interest stock, cash, property or a mixture of some or all of these categories. Investors can switch their savings from one category to another.

Suitable for: One-stop financial planning as policies can be adapted to provide more protection and less investment content, and vice-versa at different intervals, such as marriage, birth of children; insurance backing to a mortgage instead of a conventional endowment policy.

Open to: Varies; anyone; 13, 16, 18 minimum age; maximum 70, 80, 90 years.

Min–Max: £10–£50 minimum; no maximum.

Charges: Policy fee – none to £1.30 per month; initial fee 4–5 per cent deducted from premium; annual fee ¾–1 per cent.

Withdrawals: After 10 years you get the value of the units, before that there might be a capital gains tax liability; usually surrender penalty if policy encashed in early years.

Interest: Variable; accumulated within the fund.

Tax: Income tax and capital gains tax on both realised and unrealised gains paid by insurance company, reflected in underlying unit price. Proceeds tax free after 10 years; on earlier encashment higher rate taxpayers pay more.

Children: Yes, where age limits permit.

How to invest: Check performance of underlying units in specialist publications such as *Money Management* or *Planned Savings*; most companies offer this contract, phone or write for details. Independent intermediaries will be able to advise on these schemes.

Record: Insurance policy and annual unit valuation.

Money Mail Rating: ****! to *!!!!

Investor protection: Policyholders protection scheme covers 90 per cent of current unit value.

Comment: The capital gains tax liability on underlying investments is a major disadvantage compared with regular savings directly into unit trusts which roll up free of capital gains tax. As the proceeds are tax free, there can be tax planning opportunities. They are becoming increasingly popular as an alternative to endowment policies for backing an interest only mortgage. If the underlying units rise rapidly, the home loan can be repaid earlier.

With-Profits Endowment Policy

Regular savings policy for a fixed period of 10 years or more. A guaranteed sum assured is paid out on death before the end of the set term or at maturity *plus* any bonuses which the policy has earned from the underlying investments. There are two kinds of bonuses: those declared annually, "reversionary bonuses" which can never be taken away from the policy, and a "terminal bonus", which can vary, paid out at maturity.

Suitable for: Nowadays used mainly in connection with house purchase, particularly the "low cost" endowment variation; regular savings which are not required for several years.

Open to: Anyone from eight years.

Charges: Built into contract; policy fee of around £1 a month.

Min–Max: £5–£10 a month minimum; no maximum.

Withdrawals: On maturity or earlier death of life assured (usually the policyholder's, but can be another person in whom you have an "insurable", in other words financial interest). Surrender values non-existent or very low in first few years and surrender penalty remains heavy for several or many years afterwards.

Alternatively, policyholder can stop paying premiums, and make the policy "paid up" at reduced benefit level.

Interest: Variable; built into bonuses.

Tax: Income tax and capital gains tax on realised profits paid by insurance company, reflected in level of bonuses. Policy proceeds after 10 years completely tax free, but on earlier encashment higher rate taxpayers can pay more.

Children: Policies "in trust" for a child avoid inheritance tax; children over eight years can take out policy, but parent's signature required up to 18.

How to invest: Consult an insurance broker or obtain quotes direct from life offices and compare. Equitable Life, which does not pay commission, will not be included on broker quotations.

Record: Insurance policy; annual or three-yearly bonus statement.

Money Mail Rating: ****!

Investor protection: Policyholders protection scheme covers 90 per cent of benefits.

Comment: Long term endowment policies with harsh surrender policies should be avoided. Inflexible and increasingly outmoded form of savings, largely used now in connection with house purchase.

With-Profits Flexible Policy

Regular savings policy for an indefinite period which should be for at least 10 years. On death a guaranteed sum assured is paid out plus any bonuses which the policy has earned from its underlying investments. After 10 years the policy can be encashed at any time without surrender penalty at a guaranteed or part-guaranteed value. The policy is often issued as cluster of small identical policies which can each be cashed in separately.

Suitable for: Regular savings, particularly for specific targets, such as school fees, needed at least 10 years hence.

Open to: Anyone from eight years.

Min–Max: £10–£25 a month minimum; no maximum.

Charges: Built into contract; policy fee of around £1 a month.

Withdrawals: On death of life assured when guaranteed sum assured plus bonuses is paid; at guaranteed surrender value any time after 10 years; harsh surrender penalties on withdrawals before 10 years.

Interest: Variable; built into bonuses.

Tax: Income tax and capital gains tax on realised profits paid by insurance company reflected in level of bonuses. Policy proceeds after 10 years completely tax free, but on earlier encashment higher rate taxpayers can pay more.

Children: Policies "in trust" for a child avoid inheritance tax; children over eight years can take out policy, but parent's signature required up to 18.

How to invest: Consult an insurance broker or obtain quotes direct from life offices and compare.

Record: Insurance policy; annual or three-yearly bonus statement.

Money Mail Rating: ****!

Investor protection: Policyholders protection scheme covers 90 per cent of benefits.

Comment: More flexible than with-profit endowment policy which it was partially designed to replace. Cluster policies, where each bit can be cashed separately, give more flexibility still. At maturity proceeds can be left intact and a nominal premium, around £5 p.a., allows the policyholder to withdraw regular tax-free "income" from the policy, or take out tax-free money at irregular intervals.

With-Profit Bonds

Broadly the same as a with-profits endowment policy but for a lump sum investment rather than regular savings. Effectively an investment in the equity and property markets, usually with an element of gilts and cash but the fluctuations are smoothed out by the insurance companies who use their reserves to bolster the return in poor years, replenishing those reserves in good years. The bond earns a return through two types of bonus: those declared annually, "reversionary bonuses" which can never be taken away from the policy; and a "terminal bonus" which can vary, paid out at maturity.

Suitable for: Investors who want to "strip out" an income and for those who want to benefit from stockmarket/property growth without the usual fluctuations.

Open to: Anyone.

Charges: Built into contract.

Min–Max: £1,000–£5,000; no maximum.

Withdrawals: On demand at current market value, but the company can use a market value adjuster to reduce the value if market conditions are exceptionally poor. On death at current market value of units.

Charges: Initial fee usually around 5 per cent but can be reduced for larger investments. Annual fee built into contract.

Interest: none, but withdrawals can be made on a regular basis by selling units monthly, quarterly, half-yearly or annually. This can provide an income at whatever level the investor chooses.

Tax: Income tax and capital gains tax on realised profits paid by insurance company reflected in level of bonuses. Policy proceeds tax free but higher rate taxpayers can pay more.

Children: Policies "in trust" for a child avoid inheritance tax if held for seven years and could mitigate inheritance tax if held for shorter periods. Children over eight can invest but parent's signature required until 18.

How to invest: Consult a financial adviser or obtain quotes direct from life offices and compare. Look for companies with good record of bonus payments and good reserves.

Record: Insurance policy; annual bonus statement.

Money Mail Rating: ****!

Investor protection: Policyholders

protection scheme covers 90 per cent of benefits.

Comment: Can buy/sell on any business day but should be regarded as a long term investment if stripping out an income.

Temporary Annuity and "Back to Backs"

A temporary annuity is a lump sum investment which cannot be redeemed, in return for a high income for a specified period, usually five or 10 years. There is no return of capital at maturity so it is common to link the temporary annuity with a growth vehicle – usually an investment bond, unit trust or PEP – which is designed to return the original capital. This is called a "back-to-back" arrangement. A £10,000 investment can, for example, be split into a £4,000 temporary annuity to provide a high income over five years and a £6,000 PEP investment which it is hoped will grow to £10,000 over the five years.

Suitable for: Anyone looking for a high regular income who is prepared to accept the moderate degree of risk.

Open to: Anyone.

Min–Max: Usually £5,000; no maximum.

Charges: Built into contract. See appropriate sections for growth vehicles.

Interest: Fixed. Usually paid in arrears by cheque or direct to a bank account monthly, quarterly, half-yearly or annually.

Tax: Part of annuity is treated as a return of capital and tax free, the remainder treated as income and paid net of basic rate tax. Non-taxpayers can be paid gross; higher rate taxpayers pay more. See appropriate sections for growth vehicles.

Children: Possible but not particularly suitable.

How to invest: Look for advertisements in the financial press, check performances of growth vehicles in specialist publications such as *Money Management* or *Planned Savings*; phone or write to the relevant companies to ask for details before investing.

Record: Annuity contract.

Money Mail Rating: *****

Investor protection: Policyholders protection scheme covers 90 per cent of annuity benefits.

Comment: Usually a way of providing a better income than the building society but much depends on the performance of the growth vehicle. It could provide a return equal to or more than the original capital but there is a risk that it could provide less. See comment in appropriate sections for each type of growth vehicle.

Fixed Term Loan

Lump sum investment paying fixed rate interest for set period of one to 10 years. Shorter term loans available for larger sums.

Suitable for: Lock-away savings only or savings with a specific target date; five years is generally long enough to commit yourself to one form of savings. Non-taxpayers should consider Government stock on National Savings Stock Register.

Open to: Anyone aged 18 or over.

Min–Max: Varies. Minimum can be as little as £100–£500, although £1,000 more common.

Charges: None.

Withdrawals: Not permitted until end of term.

Interest: Fixed; usually paid half-yearly.

Tax: Interest paid net of tax; higher rate taxpayers pay extra. Local authorities can pay interest gross to non-taxpayers.

Children: Investment can be made on behalf of a child, but not suitable.

How to invest: Newspaper coupons, or direct from local authority (treasurer's department).

Record: Certificate.

Money Mail Rating: *****

Comment: When interest rates are falling fixed rate returns can be attractive (conversely if they are rising). The main drawback is the inflexibility. The fixed term means precisely what it says: most local authority treasurers will not permit early repayment, no matter the hardship: death is the only exception. Investors with more than £25,000 might be able to negotiate better rates.

Negotiable or Yearling Bond

Lump sum investment paying fixed rate interest for set period, normally one year, hence the name "yearling". Local authorities parcel up a selection of loan requirements into a single bond which can be bought and sold on the Stock Exchange. Investors don't identify the specific authorities behind the issue but treat it like any other fixed interest, negotiable security, such as Government stock. The bonds might be issued at a very small discount to the nominal value.

Suitable for: Any short term fixed interest investment where flexibility is required.

Open to: Anyone aged 18 or over.

Min–Max: Buy in multiples of £1,000, the minimum investment is £1,000. No maximum.

Charges: None, if bought as new issue from stockbroker and held to redemption; otherwise stockbroker's commission if you buy and sell between those dates.

Withdrawals: Hold to maturity for return of full nominal value or sell before on Stock Exchange where price can vary.

LOCAL AUTHORITY

Interest: Fixed, paid half-yearly; any interest due is added to selling price if you sell the bonds early.

Tax: Basic rate tax deducted at source but can be reclaimed by non-taxpayers; higher rate taxpayers pay extra. If you sell at a profit the gain is liable to capital gains tax.

Children: Investment can be made on behalf of a child, but not suitable.

How to invest: Through a stockbroker or bank share dealing service.

Record: Certificate.

Money Mail Rating: If held to maturity *****. If sold early ****!

Comment: Flexible: if there is any upward movement in interest rates you are not locked in; if rates fall you can stay put at bond's higher fixed rate. Compare rates with those on Government stock.

NATIONAL SAVINGS

FIRST Option Bond

Traditionally National Savings schemes have been directed at non-taxpayers, but its latest savings plan is a guaranteed investment bond, with the tax deducted at source. FIRST actually stands for Fixed Interest Rate Savings Tax-Paid. The rate is guaranteed for a year, when savers have the option of either continuing with the investment for another 12 months, at the then guaranteed interest rate, or encashing it.

Suitable for: Tax payers, although non-tax payers will be able to reclaim the tax paid on the interest.

Open to: Anyone over the age of 16. Joint holdings are accepted and trustees can hold them for personal beneficiaries.

Min–Max: £1,000–£250,000. There is no 'topping up' as each purchase is a separate bond.

Charges: None.

Withdrawals: In whole or in part at any anniversary date; no notice period is required. However, if the bond is cashed before the first anniversary, no interest will be paid. Thereafter withdrawals between anniversaries would attract half interest for the period from the previous anniversary.

Interest: Guaranteed at the time of purchase for 12 months, and added to the capital at each anniversary.

Tax: Basic rate tax is deducted at source before the interest is credited to the bond. Non-taxpayers or those liable to 20 per cent tax will be eligible for a tax refund. Higher rate taxpayers will pay more.

Children: Not until age 16.

How to invest: Direct from National Savings, Glasgow, G58 1SB. Forms are available from post offices or ring, free, 0800 88 11 88.

Record: Certificate.

Money Mail Rating: *****

Comment: After the first year, the bond is a relatively flexible addition to the National Savings repertoire. While the Government continues to need to raise funds from National Savings, the interest rate structure should remain quite attractive.

Capital Bond

Series "D"

Lump sum investment with a low minimum required. It is similar in format to National Savings Certificates but interest is paid gross, and is taxable in the hands of basic and higher rate taxpayers. Interest which is accumulated, is calculated daily and added on to the bond annually. Designed as a five year investment. The interest payments on this second series of Capital Bonds increases at a more uniform rate than the previous issue. Tax, however, has to be paid annually.

Suitable for: Non-taxpayers, children's savings and basic rate taxpayers who can leave their savings locked up for five years.

Open to: Anyone.

Min–Max: £100 – £100,000 (including Capital Bond Series "C").

Charges: None.

Withdrawals: In full, or partial withdrawals in multiples of £100 providing balance of £100 retained.

Interest: Calculated daily, accumulated before tax annually and fixed at set rates for five year term. At the end of year one: 7.2 per cent, year two: 8.2 per cent, year three: 9.7 per cent, year four: 12.13 per cent, year five: 16.78 per cent (all gross rates) giving gross compound interest rate of 10.75 per cent a year. The net return to basic rate taxpayers is 8.06 per cent.

Tax: Interest is accumulated gross, and has to be declared on your tax returns each year although payment won't be received until the bonds are encashed.

Children: Yes. Withdrawals to parents or designated trustees can be made on their behalf if under age seven and the bonds have matured.

How to invest: Application forms available at any post office.

Record: Certificate.

Money Mail Rating: *****

Comment: Definitely for savers who can last the five year course. This issue is more attractive than its predecessor. Guaranteed return will look attractive when interest rates begin to fall.

Children's Bonus Bond

A new lump sum savings for children under 16 years (who can hold them until age 21). It is a fixed rate, tax-free investment with a return of 10.9 per cent, turning £100 into £167.76, provided the bond is held for the full five years. It is important to keep the bond for five years. Interest is added at the rate of only 5 per cent a year; the real kick comes from the 40.12 per cent final bonus.

Suitable for: Children under 16 (at time of investment).

Open to: Children under 16.

Min–Max: £25–£1,000.

Charges: None.

Withdrawals: Minimum £25. One month's notice for early repayments. No interest is encashed within first year.

Interest: Fixed; 5 per cent a year plus final bonus of 47.36 per cent, making a compound annual return of 11.84 per cent if held for full five years.

Tax: Tax free.

Children: Yes.

How to invest: Application form at post offices. By anyone over the age of 16 on behalf of individual under 16.

Record: Certificate.

Money Mail Rating: *****

Comment: Very attractive return. A must for generous grandparents or relatives. But keep for five years to get maximum benefit. Suitable for gift from parent as tax-free interest does not (if it exceeds £100) have to be aggregated with that of the parent.

Deposit Bond

(withdrawn from sale on 19 November 1988)

Lump sum investment. Interest accumulates. There are surrender penalties on early encashment. Terms and conditions are guaranteed for 10 years.

Charges: None.

Withdrawals: In multiples of £50, provided £100 remains, subject to three months' notice. Interest payable reduced to half if encashed in first 12 months. Repayment forms and post-paid envelopes on request at post office. Payment by warrant, treat as cheque.

Interest: Variable, at six weeks' notice; calculated daily, credited on anniversary of purchase. Current rate: 9.25 per cent.

Tax: Not deducted, but interest is taxable and should be declared on tax return.

Children: No withdrawals if child is under seven; withdrawals after seven will require child's signature.

Money Mail Rating: *****

Comment: The return on Capital Bonds (designed to replace the Deposit Bonds) is currently lower in the first two years, and the same in the third year, so don't switch out of your Deposit Bonds unless you are definitely a long term holder.

Guaranteed Growth Bond

A new National Savings product, to be launched later in 1992, which is geared towards basic rate taxpayers. The bond will offer fixed rates of interest which are guaranteed for each year at a time. Interest, net of basic rate tax, will be added at the anniversary date. The minimum investment is to be £1,000 and the maximum £250,000. This new addition to the National Savings repertoire is expected to be very competitive with building society notice accounts, and basic rate taxpayers will need to check the rates.

Income Bond

Lump sum investment paying interest without deduction of tax at source. Interest is variable and usually competitive; it changes less frequently than bank interest rates. Surrender penalties on early encashment.

Suitable for: Retired people and others needing steady flow of income who do not need immediate access to their capital. Non-taxpayers in particular benefit from the gross interest payment and the convenience of monthly income.

Open to: Anyone.

Min–Max: Buy in multiples of £1,000; the minimum investment is £2,000, the maximum £50,000.

Charges: None.

Withdrawals: In multiples of £1,000, provided £2,000 remains invested, subject to three months' notice. Interest reduced to half if bond encashed within first 12 months. Repayment forms and pre-paid envelopes on request at post offices.

Interest: Variable, at six weeks' notice; paid on the 5th of the month direct to bank, building society or National Savings Bank, or by crossed warrant (treat as cheque). The first interest payment is made after bond held for six weeks and includes all interest due from date of investment. Rate: 9.25 per cent.

Tax: Not deducted, but interest is taxable and should be declared on tax return.

Children: Yes; but not suitable.

How to invest: Application forms available at post offices or by post from National Savings and Stock Office, Blackpool FY3 9YP, or by telephone: 0253 697333.

Record: Certificate.

Money Mail Rating: *****

Comment: Gross monthly income is attractive, but if you are a taxpayer the tax will have to be paid; pensioners close to the income ceiling limit for age allowance (see page 34) will find total income calculations easier than investments paying interest in tax paid form. Although interest is variable it is not likely to rise substantially (it can also fall): some investment providing rising income is also desirable.

Investment Account

National Savings Bank account using post office counters paying a competitive interest rate, although it changes less frequently than other banks' interest rates. Interest, which does not have tax deducted at source, accumulates.

Suitable for: Non-taxpayers including children who do not require immediate access to their funds; for irregular savings of different amounts.

Open to: Anyone.

Min–Max: Any amount of £5 or more for each deposit. Maximum investment of £25,000 does not include interest credited to the account.

Charges: None.

Withdrawals: One month's notice from date application received at National Savings Bank HQ paid by crossed warrant (treat as cheque) or cash at named post office. Repayment forms and pre-paid envelopes on request at post offices.

Interest: Variable; automatically credited to accounts on 31 December. Bank books should be sent to National Savings Bank, Glasgow G58 1SB, to have interest entered. Annual interest statement available on request. Current rate: 8.5 per cent.

Tax: Not deducted, but interest is taxable and should be declared on tax return. The National Savings Bank has to inform the Inland Revenue of interest paid on each account.

Children: Yes, but no withdrawals for under sevens; investment can be made by parents as trustee when same conditions apply, withdrawals after seven will require child's signature as well. Relatives or friends can open account in child's name; no withdrawals under the age of seven, afterwards child can withdraw on own signature.

How to invest: Application form at post office; fill in form at post office for subsequent deposits. "Save-by-Post" service available: write to National Savings Bank, Glasgow G58 1SB or ring free 0800 100 100. Dividends from shares and Government stock can be credited directly to the account.

Record: Bank book.

Money Mail Rating: *****

Comment: Not a substitute for a high interest cheque book account; judge on investment rather than banking merits; gross interest payments attractive. The moderately complicated withdrawal procedure prevents casual usage, for example, by children for whom the account is particularly suitable. It takes longer to get interest credited in January than at any other time of the year, and there is nothing to be gained by sending the bank book off so early.

Ordinary Account

Two-tiered bank account using post office counters offering modest interest, partly tax free, easy access to funds and some banking services.

Suitable for: Day-to-day money management of people who either have no bank current account or are frequent users of the post office, for example to draw a pension or other benefits. Higher rate taxpayers who benefit from the partly tax-free interest.

Open to: Anyone.

Min–Max: £5–£10,000.

Charges: None.

Withdrawals: Up to £100 on demand at any post office, but if over £50 withdrawn bank book kept for checking. "Regular Customer Account" permits up to £250 in cash a day at one chosen post office where you have been a customer for at least six months. Written applications required for larger withdrawals; forms and pre-paid envelopes on request at post offices.

Bills normally paid at the post office e.g. TV licence, road tax, totalling not more than £250 at a time can be paid directly from the account.

Interest: Provided the account is open for the full calendar year, investors earn a guaranteed 5 per cent for each calendar month that there is £500 or more in the account, otherwise 2.5 per cent. No interest is payable on month in which investment or withdrawal is made.

Tax: Not deducted at source and as partly taxable should be declared, in full, on tax return. The first £70 of interest is tax free (capital required £1,400).

Children: Yes, but no withdrawals for under sevens; relatives or friends can open an account in child's name but no withdrawals under seven, afterwards child can withdraw on own signature.

How to invest: Application form at post office; fill in form at post office for subsequent deposits.

Record: Bank book.

Money Mail Rating: *****

Comment: Alternative to bank current account for people who want instant record of transactions. If you cannot keep £500 in the account, building society ordinary account will pay more even if interest paid net of tax; with £500 or more building society cheque or cash card account will usually pay more and offer some banking services too. Higher rate taxpayers no longer benefit from keeping their maximum £1,400 (for tax-free interest). Compare 5 per cent with 5.7 per cent from the National Savings Investment account after deducting 40 per cent income tax.

5th Issue Index-Linked Certificates

Lump sum investment, popularly known as "Granny Bonds", for small to medium-sized amounts which will both grow in line with increases in the cost of living, as measured by the Retail Prices Index, and earn guaranteed interest each year. Certificates have to be held for 12 months to qualify for index-linking. The repayment value of certificates is published each month in the press and listed in post offices. This latest issue has a low scale of annual bonuses, although the final compound bonus is attractive.

Suitable for: Most investors when rate of inflation looks set to increase, but more suitable for higher rate taxpayers than non-taxpayers.

Open to: Anyone.

Min–Max: One unit of £25; maximum £10,000 (400 units). This is in addition to any other holdings, index-linked and conventional, of National Savings Certificates. A further £10,000 from matured issues of other certificates (index-linked or conventional) and Yearly Plan can be invested in this issue.

Charges: None.

Withdrawals: Eight working days' notice required. Repayment form and pre-paid envelope available at post office. Partial withdrawals in £25 units permitted. If withdrawn in first year, money back only.

Interest: Guaranteed for five years. Index-linking is added at the end of the first year on the anniversary of purchase and thereafter the value of certificates moves in line with changes in the Retail Price Index. Extra, guaranteed interest is added at the end of the third year (0.5 per cent), fourth year (1 per cent) and fifth year (2 per cent). The compound annual interest rate is 4.5 per cent, on top of index-linking, over five years. After year five, index-linking will continue and variable rate interest will be paid.

Tax: Free of income tax and capital gains tax and need not be declared on tax return.

Children: Yes, but children have to be aged over seven before certificates can be encashed other than in exceptional circumstances, such as great hardship. Certificates held in trust do not count towards the individual's own maximum investment.

How to invest: Most post offices and banks have application forms. Quote your holder's number if you have one.

Record: Certificate. Holder's card which has registered number under which all certificates are held is issued at first purchase of any certificate. This number is quoted on all certificates of whatever issue is bought.

Money Mail Rating: *****

Investor protection: Guaranteed by Government.

Comment: Higher rate taxpayers should top up their holding of tax-free certificates. Provided certificates are held for 12 months, a fairly flexible form of savings.

37th Issue Savings Certificates

Lump sum investment for modest amounts which should be held for five years to obtain the maximum benefits, which are tax free, although easier withdrawals are possible.

Suitable for: Long term savings, gifts to children. Particularly attractive to higher rate taxpayers; non-taxpayers should avoid.

Open to: Anyone.

Min–Max: £25 (one unit); maximum £10,000, but savers of matured issues of savings certificates, including index-linked certificates, can reinvest up to £10,000 of the proceeds into this issue.

Charges: None.

Withdrawals: Any number of units. Repayment form and envelope available at post office, allow two weeks for repayment either by warrant (treat as cheque) or cash at the post office.

Interest: If held for the full five years, the compound annual rate of interest works out at 8 per cent a year. No interest is paid until the end of the first year, thereafter it is paid at three-monthly intervals. At the end of year 1, 5.5 per cent is added; 6.2 per cent at the end of year 2; 8 per cent year 3; 9.4 per cent year 4; and 11 per cent at the end of year 5. Investors cashing in "reinvested certificates" in the first year will receive interest, at the rate of 5.5 per cent a year, for each complete three-month period.

Tax: The interest is tax free and need not be declared on your tax return.

Children: Suitable for gifts to children; certificates in a child's name cannot be encashed until child is seven.

How to invest: At your local post office. If it is a second or subsequent purchase of certificates (any issue) your holder's number card.

Record: Certificate. If it is your first purchase of certificates you will be given a holder's number card which covers all future purchases of certificates you might make. Quote this number for subsequent purchases or any withdrawals.

Money Mail Rating: *****

Investor protection: Guaranteed by Government.

Comment: Higher rate taxpayers should keep their National Savings Certificates topped up. If you think interest rates are going to fall, exercise the option to convert matured holdings into the 36th Issue. Theoretically if you think interest rates will rise in the next five years, then the variable General Extension Rate interest earned on mature issues offers more flexibility for switching. In practice, the rate is so low (5.01 per cent) it is not worth keeping any money at this rate. So cash in your old certificates, particularly as the Government seems reluctant to issue higher-paying new issues of NS Certificates.

Premium Bond

In effect, a money-back lottery ticket. About £2,100 million is invested in Premium Bonds. Once a month ERNIE (Electronic Random Number Indicator Equipment) picks out at random over 199,000 £1 bond numbers which will win prizes ranging from £50 to a "jack-pot" of £250,000. In addition there are weekly prizes of £25,000, £50,000 and £100,000. Every prize winner is notified by post; the post office lists all the winning numbers and big prize numbers are published in the press.

Suitable for: Anyone wanting a flutter without losing his or her stake money. Tax-free winning, if any, attractive for higher rate taxpayers. An alternative to cash gifts.

Open to: Anyone.

Min–Max: £1 bonds sold in multiples of £10, minimum investment £100; maximum £10,000. Bonds have to be held for three clear calendar months before being eligible for the draw. Winners of £50 Premium Bond prizes will be able to reinvest their prize warrants despite the £100 minimum transaction. For children under 16, the minimum purchase is £10.

Charges: None.

Withdrawals: Money back only. Partial withdrawals in £10 multiples allowed. Repayment forms and pre-paid envelopes available at post offices. Allow eight working days before repayment either by crossed warrant (treat as cheque) or cash at post office.

Interest: None. The prize fund is currently calculated at 6.5 per cent of total money invested in Premium Bonds.

Tax: Prizes free of income tax and capital gains tax and need not be declared on tax return.

Children: Under the age of 16 bonds must be bought by parent, guardian or grandparent to whom any prize money will be paid.

Record: Bond which is issued with individual holder's numbers.

Money Mail Rating: *****

Investor protection: Guaranteed by Government.

Comment: The odds on winning any prize are 11,000 to 1 – and there are many more £50–£100 prizes than there are big ones. A single bond in the minimum multiple of £10 has as much chance of winning as one from a block of £10,000. There are unclaimed prizes worth £9.76 million at 1 April 1992. Are any of them yours?

Save As You Earn (SAYE)

4th Issue Series "C" Share Option Scheme

Regular monthly savings linked to a company share option scheme. Employees are offered the option to buy shares at a price fixed at the start of the five year savings period which cannot be less than 80 per cent of market value. Employees invest a set amount each month in the SAYE scheme. At the end of five years they can either use the money to exercise the share option or take the money. They can leave the money invested for another two years to obtain the higher bonus BUT they will then lose the share option entitlement. However, some employers offer a seven year share option plan when the share option can then be exercised.

Interest in the SAYE accumulates tax free. In addition there is a bonus of 15 months' payments tax free at the end of five years, or 30 months' if you leave the savings in for the next two years. From 1 October the bonus is cut from 15 to 12.5 months and from 30 to 25 respectively, reducing the return to 7.5 per cent for five years and 7.83 per cent for seven.

Suitable for: Employees who want to build up a share stake in their company.

Open to: Employers running a scheme fix the eligibility rules, usually determined by length of service with the company. Employees may have more than one share option SAYE scheme, provided the overall monthly contribution does not exceed the maximum.

Min–Max: £10 a month minimum, £250 a month maximum.

Charges: None.

Withdrawals: No partial withdrawals. Reduced interest rate penalties on early withdrawal; no interest in year one; years two to five, 5 per cent. If you die, your executor can either take the amount saved or buy shares at the option price.

Interest: Fixed. Including the bonus is equivalent to 8.86 per cent over five years; including the enlarged bonus, the rate over seven years is equivalent to 9.15 per cent. It is accumulated.

Tax: Tax free. Once the share option is exercised, dividends are taxable and there is a potential gains tax liability, based on the actual purchase price of the shares, when you sell them.

Children: No.

How to invest: You will be invited by your employer to participate in the scheme.

Record: Certificate.

Money Mail Rating: ***** until the share option is exercised.

Investor protection: SAYE is guaranteed by the Government.

Comment: A useful way of hedging your bets. If the company's shares have risen since you were granted the option, then you exercise the option and buy the share at the lower price fixed when you began savings. You will have a built-in profit. However, if your company has been less successful and the share price is actually lower than the option price, then take the SAYE proceeds as cash.

Yearly Plan

Regular savings plan for one year at fixed rate of interest; plan then converted to a certificate and if held for further four years it earns higher fixed rate of interest. A new yearly plan can be taken out each year: the interest rate on subsequent issues might be fixed at different rates. Interest is reinvested and is tax free.

Suitable for: Most investors wishing to save regularly who are not put off by its superficial complexity. To get the maximum benefit the plan should not be held for five years in all so savings should be for a build-up of capital or medium term target where it is important to know what your savings will be worth then.

Open to: Anyone.

Min–Max: In multiples of £5, minimum £20 a month, maximum £200.

Charges: None.

Withdrawals: No partial withdrawals; 14 days' notice; repayment form and pre-paid envelopes available at post office. No interest is payable if plan encashed within first 12 months.

Interest: Fixed. If held for full five years 8.5 per cent a year. Rates are lower if you encash the plan earlier: 5 per cent p.a. if held for less than two years; 9 per cent if held for more than two but less than four years. If six or fewer monthly payments are made, the interest rate is 3 per cent p.a.

Tax: Free of income tax and capital gains tax and need not be declared on tax return.

Children: Parents can invest on behalf of a child under seven, but no withdrawals until aged seven.

How to invest: Application forms at post office, but payment must be by standing order.

Record: Certificate.

Money Mail Rating: *****

Investor protection: Guaranteed by Government.

Comment: Fixed rate attractive when interest rates in general are falling. This savings plan is not as popular as it sometimes deserves to be.

Building Society Account

A handful of building societies now have branches offshore, principally in the Isle of Man, which enable them to pay interest gross to UK investors. There is a range of accounts available including Instant Access, Notice and Term Shares. They tend to have higher minimum investments but otherwise are identical to mainland accounts but interest is paid without deduction of tax.

Suitable for: Non-taxpayers including non-working wives who need gross interest to offset against their new personal tax allowance, children and other non-taxpayers. Taxpayers wishing to defer their tax liability on the interest.

Open to: Anyone.

Min–Max: Varies from £1,000 to £5,000. No maximum.

Charges: None.

Withdrawals: Depends on type of account: instant access on demand; notice accounts, usually three months; term shares, one or more years.

Interest: Variable; paid gross either half-yearly or annually. Often marginally higher than similar "onshore" account.

Tax: Interest is paid without deduction of tax.

Children: Yes. Parent's signature required for under sevens.

How to invest: Consult your local branch. Most large societies operate offshore accounts for UK residents.

Record: Passbook.

Money Mail Rating: *****

Investor protection: Societies' offshore operations are outside the scope of the Investors Protection Act, but under the Building Societies Act 1986, societies are legally bound to bail out any subsidiary which gets into trouble.

Comment: These accounts were designed to appeal to non-working wives in the wake of independent taxation, and set up, in the main, before the 1990 Budget which abolished composite rate tax from April 1991. Now that societies in the UK are able to offer gross interest to non-taxpayers most investors will probably prefer to stay "onshore", although the offshore rates are often a little higher. Some societies (National & Provincial, Woolwich and Yorkshire) allow you to choose your annual interest payment date either side of 5 April to suit your tax position.

Do not confuse these offshore building society accounts with those designed for non-UK residents only which have always been able to offer gross interest to people not liable to UK tax.

Currency Fund

Equivalent to bank deposit account in a foreign currency of your own choice, although the investment method is to buy and sell shares in the fund. It is possible to own shares in a currency fund denominated in any of the major world currencies and other less obvious ones such as the Danish kroner, Singapore dollar or Irish punt, and ECU (European Currency Unit). Within the same management group it is possible to switch from one currency to another.

Suitable for: Non-taxpayers; investors taking a view on currency values; future holiday funds.

Open to: Anyone aged 18 or over.

Min–Max: Varies; commonly £1,000. No maximum.

Charges: No initial fee; annual fee ¾–1¼ per cent.

Withdrawals: Up to seven days.

Interest: Variable; paid gross half-yearly or annually in either foreign currency or sterling if fund "distributor" fund. Reinvested if "accumulation" fund.

Tax: With a distributor fund the income is paid gross and UK taxpayers must declare and pay income tax on the distribution. With an accumulation, the interest is rolled up in the fund without deduction of tax, but when the UK investor realises his profit he will pay income tax on the entire capital gain (which includes any currency appreciations as well as reinvested income).

Children: Not suitable.

How to invest: Check investment performance in specialist publications such as *Money Management* and *Money International*. Prices and addresses of management companies quoted in Offshore Funds page of the *Financial Times*.

Record: Share certificate.

Money Mail Rating: **!!! to *!!!!

Investor protection: Regulations have changed from an investor protection point of view. Offshore tax havens such as the Isle of Man, the Channel Islands and Bermuda are now designated territories which means that each has a supervisory system similar to the UK's, including a compensation scheme. Individual funds which are marketed in this country have to be recognised. Either the management company must belong to a regulatory body (for example LAUTRO) or the individual fund regulated by the Securities and Investments Board.

Comment: As managers can obtain a higher, if not the maximum interest rate available on the larger sums (the investors' pooled shareholdings) they have to invest, a single currency fund is an attractive alternative to an individual foreign currency deposit account.

"Managed" currency funds are also available where the investment manager chooses a basket of currencies for you, switching between them depending on the relative outlook for each currency.

High Interest Cheque Account

Interest bearing current account, usually with minimum starting investment, at a bank or branch of UK bank in the Channel Islands or Isle of Man. It operates in the same way as a domestic high interest cheque account but with the interest paid gross, not net. Most banks stipulate a minimum cheque withdrawal; direct debits and standing orders may be permitted; no overdraft facilities.

Suitable for: It is a complementary account to a current account; the gross payment of interest may have cash flow attractions to taxpayers, who will pay the tax later.

Open to: Anyone aged 18 or over (20 in Jersey).

Min–Max: £1,000–£2,000–£2,500. No maximum.

Charges: Limited number of free cheques at most banks, subsequent ones commonly cost 50p each.

Withdrawals: With a few exceptions, minimum cheque withdrawal £200–£250.

Interest: Variable, paid into account quarterly, half-yearly or annually without deduction of tax.

Tax: UK investors declare and pay income tax on the interest.

Children: Not unless account held in adult's name.

How to invest: Obtain address of offshore subsidiary from your local branch of Bank of Scotland, Barclays, Cater Allen, Lloyds, Midland, National Westminster and TSB.

Record: Bank statements.

Money Mail Rating: *****

Investor protection: No deposit protection scheme, so it is essential to choose a bank which is a subsidiary of a UK bank or well known internationally.

Comment: Consider it as an alternative to a domestic high interest current account or instant access building society account.

Managed Currency Fund

Lump sum investment through the purchase of shares in a professionally managed fund based outside the UK which invests in a range of cash deposits and other monetary investments (called "instruments") such as bills, in a variety of foreign currencies. It effectively operates like a unit trust with the hoped-for gain coming not from appreciation in equity prices, but from one currency rising in value against another.

Suitable for: Investors who want to hold assets abroad, but do not want to select which currency to hold their money in; non-taxpayers, but there are only marginal tax advantages for UK taxpayers.

OFFSHORE

Open to: Anyone aged 18 or over.

Min–Max: Usually £1,000; no maximum.

Charges: Initial fee of 3–4 per cent; annual fee ¾–1¼ per cent.

Withdrawals: Up to seven days.

Interest: Variable, paid either half-yearly or annually if the fund has "distributor" status; or accumulated in an accumulation fund. In both cases paid without deduction of tax at source, but the tax treatment differs.

Tax: Offshore currency funds are either "distributor" funds or "accumulation" funds. With a distributor fund, the income is paid out gross and UK taxpayers declare and pay income tax on the distribution. With an accumulation fund, the interest is rolled up in the fund without deduction of tax, but when the UK investor realises his profit he will pay income tax on the entire capital gain (which includes any currency appreciation as well as reinvested income) he has made.

Children: Must be held on behalf of a child in adult's name.

How to invest: Consult specialist publications such as *Money Management* for performance record and companies' addresses. Prices and addresses are also listed in the Offshore Funds page of the *Financial Times*.

Record: Share certificate.

Money Mail Rating: **!!! to *!!!!

Investor protection: Regulations have changed from an investor protection point of view. Offshore tax havens such as the Isle of Man, the Channel Islands and Bermuda are now designated territories which means that each has a supervisory system similar to the UK's, including a compensation scheme. Individual funds which are marketed in this country have to be recognised. Either the management company must belong to a regulatory body (such as LAUTRO) or the individual fund regulated by the Securities and Investments Board.

Comment: Check whether the fund has "distributor" status or not. Among UK banks and unit trust management companies with offshore funds are Guinness Flight, Hill Samuel, MIM Britannia, Old Court (a Rothschild company), Prudential, N. M. Schroder and TSB.

Term Account

Lump sum, fixed term, fixed interest rate investment with money tied up for one to five years, in a bank or deposit taker in the Channel Islands or Isle of Man. Interest is paid without deduction of tax.

Suitable for: Anyone taking a view that interest rates elsewhere will fall.

Open to: Anyone.

Min–Max: £100–£5,000 minimum; there may be a maximum, typically £50,000.

Charges: None.

Withdrawals: At end of term, other than in exceptional circumstances, but interest rate then usually reduced.

Interest: Fixed; paid without deduction of tax; higher rates sometimes negotiable for larger sums. For shorter term investments, interest payable at maturity, otherwise half-yearly or annually.

Tax: UK investors declare and pay income tax on the interest.

Children: Not suitable.

How to invest: Obtain address of offshore subsidiaries from UK banks.

Record: Statement.

Money Mail Rating: *****

Investor protection: No compensation scheme, so it is essential to choose a bank which is a subsidiary of UK bank or deposit taker.

Comment: Short term cash flow attractions for taxpayers who defer the tax liability. Compare the gross equivalent interest rates of the fixed interest investments where interest has tax deducted at source.

Unit Trust

Lump sum investment in a professionally managed pool of money which is invested in a wide spread of shares, stock and other assets. It is similar to a UK authorised unit trust, but because it is based offshore, comes under different regulations. Funds from "designated" territories – the Channel Islands, Bermuda and the Isle of Man – now operate under a similar system to the UK's if the funds are marketed over here, and a similar compensation scheme applies.

UCITS have been available since October 1989. The acronym stands for Undertaking for Collective Investments in Transferable Securities and is the invention of the European Commission to cover all forms of collective investments, such as unit trusts, offered by individual Common Market countries to investors in EC member states. Provided individual investment schemes, such as a unit trust, match the rules of a UCITS, then it can be marketed freely.

UCITS marketed in this country have to be registered, and follow the UK's investor protection rules, but there is not a compensation scheme to fall back upon.

UCITS can invest in transferable securities such as shares and fixed interest investments, and put up to 5 per cent of their funds into other collective investment schemes.

Suitable for: Investors wishing to transfer funds outside the UK or to keep foreign-earned assets abroad.

Open to: Anyone.

Min–Max: Varies. Commonly £500–£1,000. No maximum.

Charges: Initial fee of 5–8½ per cent; annual fee of ½–1 per cent.

Withdrawals: Usually on demand at market price, sometimes one month's notice.

Interest: Variable; paid as dividend half-yearly without deduction of tax.

Tax: UK investors declare and pay income tax on the dividend and are liable to capital gains tax on profits at disposal.

Children: Not suitable.

How to invest: Check specialist publications such as *Money Management* for performance record. Prices and addresses of management companies listed in Offshore Funds page of *Financial Times*.

Record: Certificate.

Money Mail Rating: **!!! to !!!!!

Investor protection: It is important to remember that the investor protection rules (see page 84) for both UCITS and offshore unit trusts only apply to those funds which are marketed in the UK, either by a financial adviser or the management company itself, say, through press advertising. If you apply direct to the management company yourself, wherever it is based, they will not apply. It will always be sensible to stick to investments run by subsidiaries of established UK companies or those which are well known internationally.

Comment: From the pure investment point of view for a UK taxpayer there is little to choose between a UK unit trust and an offshore one. Much more depends on the motive or need to keep assets offshore.

If you have a pensions problem, such as a suspected miscalculation of a pension or any other unresolved dispute with your existing or former pension scheme, then the Occupational Pensions Advisory Service can help. It is a charity advised by leading people from the pensions industry, and its services are free to pensioners and employees who have exhausted any discussions with the company pension scheme. It will not advise on any current pensions decision – such as to stay with a company pension scheme or opt for a new personal pension plan – you might be considering. Occupational Pensions Advisory Service, 11 Belgrave Road, London SW1V 1RB, Tel: 071-233 8080. A Pensions Ombudsman scheme to cover all aspects of the pensions industry was launched in spring 1991. Tel: 071-834 9144.

Additional Voluntary Contributions

Tax-free regular savings plan, for at least five years either linked to your company pension scheme or quite separate from it. Your total contributions to your pension scheme and AVC must not exceed 15 per cent of your earnings. All employees who belong to a company pension scheme have the right to make AVC contributions and since October 1987, all employees who belong to a company pension scheme can select their own "free-standing" AVC, outside the firm's pension scheme.

Suitable for: Anyone who began their pension planning late; last minute boost to retirement income; higher rate taxpayers trying to reduce their tax bill.

Open to: Anyone who belongs to an approved company pension scheme.

Min–Max: £5–£10 a month; maximum 15 per cent of your earnings, including mainstream pension scheme contributions on up to a maximum salary of £75,000.

Charges: Built into life assurance schemes; none with building society AVCs.

Withdrawals: At retirement, as pension and cash commutation with contracts taken out before 17 March 1987; no commutation permitted on AVCs begun since then. If you change jobs, your existing contributions continue to roll up to provide you with a pension based on their value at retirement. If you die before retirement, a full refund plus interest is made.

Tax: Premiums get tax relief in full; the pension is treated as earned income, and the commuted cash sum is tax free.

Children: No.

How to invest: Your pension scheme manager will advise you of the company's own AVC scheme. If choosing your own free stand (FSAVC) scheme check performance of underlying company in the specialist magazines.

Record: Annual statement of contributions, AVC value to date.

Money Mail Rating: Depending on underlying investments ***** to ****!

Investor protection: Policyholders Protection Act covers 90 per cent of benefits promised by UK authorised insurers provided they are not "excessive". Building society investments covered by building society compensation scheme.

Comment: Best way of boosting future retirement income. If you have been contributing to your company pension scheme for a long time and can expect a pension of two-thirds of final salary or close to that amount, there will not be any point in paying AVCs as your pension, irrespective of how much you have paid towards it, must not exceed two-thirds of final salary. Your pension scheme manager should alert you to this possibility. If you have "over-funded" new rules permit the excess AVCs to be refunded less tax of 35 per cent for basic rate taxpayers, 48 per cent for higher rate taxpayers.

Personal Pension Plan

A regular savings scheme for pension provision available from July 1988 which can be bought by employees who do not belong to a company pension scheme; employees who belong to a company pension scheme will also have the option of taking out a personal pension plan instead. Personal pension plans are in effect a refinement of and will have many features in common with Self-Employed Retirement Annuities. The totally new feature is the concessions which will be available to employees taking out a personal pension plan instead of remaining in the State Earnings Related Pension Scheme (SERPS) to which all employees not in a company pension scheme automatically belong. Employers, if they wish, can contribute to your personal pension plan. Building societies and unit trust groups are able to offer personal pensions, as well as insurance companies.

Suitable for: Younger, mobile employees, particularly if their company agrees to contribute to the personal pension. Self-employed. House purchase with a pensions mortgage. Older employees who are currently in a company pension scheme unlikely to benefit.

Open to: Self-employed and employees not in a company pension scheme.

Min–Max: With a few plans can be as low as £10 a month (which won't buy you much pension). Maximum is effectively £10,500 (up to age 35), more if older, as contributions limited to earnings of £75,000. In addition to your contributions, and possibly your employer's, the Government, in some circumstances, will make a contribution too. Employees leaving SERPS to take out a personal pension plan will get the National Insurance rebate for contracting out of SERPS. In addition there will be a 2 per cent incentive (again of upper tier earnings) for the tax year 1992–93 paid into the Pension Plan. It will be 1 per cent for those over 30 afterwards.

Charges: Investment in the first one to two years often in "initial" or "capital" units carrying charges of around 7.5 per cent; thereafter around 0.75 per cent a year.

Withdrawals: A pension may be taken from age 50. Cash commutation of 20–25 per cent of individual pension "pot".

Interest: Variable; reinvested.

Tax: Tax relief in full on contributions of 17½ per cent of earnings up to age 35, 20 per cent of earnings from 36–45, 25 per cent from 46–50, 30 per cent from 51–55, 35 per cent from 56–60 and 40 per cent from 61 years. Pension taxed as income; lump sum tax free.

Children: No.

Record: Policy and statement.

Money Mail Rating: ***** to ****!

Investor protection: Personal pension plans come under the investor protection framework of the Financial Services Act: separate arrangements exist made for those types of schemes, such as invest in building society deposits, which are not covered by the Act.

Comment: Employees who are not in a company pension scheme should consider this option carefully. Employees who belong to a company pension scheme should compare the combined contributions level made to the company pension scheme by them and their employers with the proposed contribution level to a personal pension plan. A significantly lower contribution level will almost certainly mean a lower pension.

Self-Employed Retirement Annuity

Regular savings or intermittent lump savings out of tax-free income towards a retirement pension for anyone who does not belong to an occupational pension scheme, a category which includes employees who do not belong to a company pension scheme as well as the self-employed. These contracts ceased to be available from 1 July 1988 when they were replaced by the new Personal Pension Plan (see page 87), but it is still possible to continue with an existing scheme and make additional contributions to it. Contributions to retirement annuities are invested in insurance type contracts schemes and grow by the addition of bonuses; others resemble unit-linked insurance. At retirement date, the holder has an "open-market" option to choose the highest available annuity, not necessarily the one provided by the company.

Suitable for: Self-employed and those not in a company pension scheme; employees who have additional source of income not covered by the company pension scheme. House purchase with a pension mortgage. Late pension planning.

Open to: Only to those who took out plan before 1 July 1988, and who wish to either increase their contributions or carry forward payments for previous six years.

Min–Max: Regular premiums £10 a month, single premium £500–£1,000. Maximum depends on your earnings and age. It is 17.5 per cent up to age 50, 20 per cent for 51–55, 22.5 per cent for 56–60 and 27.5 per cent for 61 and over.

Charges: Built into the contract with with-profits type insurances; initial fees of 5 per cent and annual ¾ per cent with unit-linked schemes.

Withdrawals: As a pension starting at age 60–75 (the age must be specified at the outset), earlier dates are permitted for special occupations such as money market brokers and footballers; up to around one-third of pension fund can be taken as a tax-free cash lump sum but for contracts taken out from 17 March 1987 the sum must not exceed £150,000.

Interest: Variable; reinvested in the pension fund.

Tax: Tax relief in full on the premiums given to the level appropriate to your age. You can carry forward contributions, and obtain tax relief, for the preceding six years and forward one year. The cash lump sum is tax free; the pension is taxed as earned income.

Children: No.

How to invest: Consult an insurance broker or ask individual companies for a quote.

Record: Pensions policy and statements.

Money Mail Rating: ***** to ****!

Investor protection: Policies issued by UK insurance companies are covered by compensation scheme providing 90 per cent of benefits provided they are not "excessive". Intermediaries selling pensions policies must belong to a self-regulatory organisation.

Transfer Plan

(or *Section 32 Buy Out Bond*)

All job changers now have the choice of leaving their deferred pension with the ex-employer or taking the transfer value of their pension entitlement to either their new company or to the insurance market to purchase a Transfer Plan, often known as a Buy Out Bond. Some companies might only permit such a transfer in respect of pension rights built up since January 1986, when they were compelled to offer job leavers this choice. The money is invested in an individual account and at retirement age, 60–70, is used to buy either a fixed or rising income pension.

Suitable for: Anyone changing jobs who belongs to an occupational pension scheme, or who is made redundant.

Open to: See above.

Min–Max: In practice £1,000; no maximum.

Charges: Included in the investment.

Withdrawals: At retirement only and as a pension only, apart from a tax-free lump sum cash commutation of up to about one-quarter of your final pension fund.

Interest: Variable, and accumulated within the pension fund.

Tax: Cash sum commuted is tax free, and the pension in payment is taxed as earned income.

Children: No.

How to invest: Consult your outgoing pension scheme manager for details of your pension transfer value. Some companies prefer to handle the arrangements; others will be more amenable to accepting your choice of company for the Buy Out Bond. An insurance broker, or possibly the pension scheme manager at your new job will also be able to give advice. Most insurance companies market Buy Out Bonds including Equitable Life, Legal & General, London & Manchester, London Life, NPI, Scottish Widows, Standard Life, Sun Life.

Record: Policy document.

Money Mail Rating: ****!

Investor protection: Policyholders Protection Act covers 90 per cent of insurance benefits provided they are not "excessive". This only applies to authorised UK insurance companies.

Comment: Buy Out Bonds nearly always provide a higher pension than a deferred pension with your former employer. In many ways, the Personal Pension Plan can be used as a more flexible alternative.

Business Expansion Scheme and Fund

Lump sum investment in either a single venture or in a fund which invests in several Business Expansion Schemes. Tax relief in full is given on investments up to £40,000 a year provided the shares are not sold for five years, and the proceeds are also free from capital gains tax. Most BES are now property-linked to assured tenancies in conjunction with housing associations or universities. There is usually an "assured" exit route at the end of the five year period, which will provide the cash to buy the properties from the BES. Returns for higher rate taxpayers are in 14 per cent league. The aim of other BES companies is to obtain a quotation on the Unlisted Securities Market which will provide the market place for share disposals. Otherwise, the company's sponsors or BES fund manager will try to find a buyer for your shares.

Open to: Anyone who is neither an employee nor a connection of the company.

Suitable for: Long term investors only. Higher rate taxpayers and investors wanting to back new companies. A BES fund spreads the risk.

Min–Max: £500 in a single BES company; £2,000 in a BES fund. Maximum is £40,000 in each tax year, although it is possible to carry back £5,000 of that year's £40,000 into the preceding tax year.

Charges: These vary widely. Most fund managers charge an initial fee of 2–7 per cent, and may impose an annual management charge of 1 per cent. If you are investing directly into a BES company, check the charges in the prospectus which the company must pay to the sponsor (for administration, handling the issue etc.) which can range from 6 to 27 per cent.

Withdrawals: If you can find a buyer of your shares, at any time. However, you will lose both the income tax and capital gains tax concessions if you sell before five years. After five years, it will also be easier to sell the shares.

Interest: Usually none; very few companies will be ready to pay dividends within the initial five year period.

Tax: You can invest up to £40,000 a year in a BES company or fund and obtain tax relief in full on that investment provided the shares are held for five years. You can carry back into the preceding tax year 50 per cent of any investment, up to a maximum carryback of £5,000, made between 6 April and 5 October of the current tax year. Shares bought after 18 March 1986 are free of capital gains tax on disposal after five years; losses cannot be offset against other gains.

Children: Not suitable.

How to invest: Most BES companies and funds tend to raise money in the few months preceding the end of the tax year; issue details are usually covered in the press and specialist publications such as the *BES magazine* and *Investors Chronicle*. Only deal in companies with well-known sponsors and established fund managers.

Record: Share certificate in BES company; certificate of participation in a BES fund.

Money Mail Rating: ***!! to !!!!!

Investor protection: Sponsors and fund managers must belong to one of the self-regulatory organisations and investors are covered by the appropriate compensation scheme, maximum £48,000.

Comment: Assured tenancy BES are generally considered "safer" than those backing industrial or commercial activities. If you are going for a company rather than a fund, it is desirable to spread the risk with more than one investment. This is the last year to invest in a BES. The scheme is to be withdrawn at the end of 1993.

Investment Trusts

An investment collective: individual shareholders' funds are pooled and invested in a professionally managed well-spread portfolio of stocks and shares. Unlike a unit trust, an investment trust is a publicly quoted company whose shares are quoted on the Stock Exchange and rise and fall in value according to demand. Sometimes shares are traded above the "net asset value", the underlying market value of underlying portfolio of shares, in which case they stand at a "premium"; often they stand at a "discount", that is are traded below the net asset value. Traditionally investment trusts had very general portfolios; nowadays many of them specialise in certain geographical areas, such as Europe or Japan.

Suitable for: Long term investors; smaller lump sums; investors wanting to concentrate on one specific investment area.

Open to: Anyone.

Min–Max: Theoretically no minimum, but stockbroker's commission makes investment in amounts below £500 less worthwhile. No maximum.

Charges: Stockbroker's commission. Commission fees now 1.5–1.6 per cent, less for deals over £7,000–£8,000 often with a minimum of £20–£25.

Withdrawals: Sell shares in any amount through a stockbroker at current market price. You will receive your money in two to three weeks.

Interest: Variable, called "dividend" and usually paid half-yearly by cheque or direct to bank account.

Tax: Interest is paid net of basic rate tax, the amount deducted known as "tax credit" can be reclaimed by non-taxpayers; higher rate taxpayers pay more. Although investment trust itself not liable to capital gains tax, gains made by investment trust company shareholders are liable to capital gains tax.

Children: Shares bought for a child must be registered in adult's name.

How to invest: Through a stockbroker or bank's share dealing service after asking their advice; consult specialist publications for up-to-date commentary and views on the 200 or so investment trusts available. Unlike unit trusts, investment trusts cannot be sold by off-the-page advertisements.

Record: Share certificate.

Money Mail Rating: ***!! to *!!!!

Investor protection: Most management companies to belong to Investment Management Regulatory Organisation (IMRO) and investors are covered by its compensation scheme, maximum £48,000.

Comment: Investment trusts are more complicated than unit trusts because the share price can move independently of underlying market value of portfolio, but in the last 10 years investment trusts, on average, have proved more rewarding than unit trusts.

Investment Trust Savings Scheme

Regular savings scheme for unlimited period into an investment trust, monthly contributions collected and invested at advantageous dealing costs. In addition there is also a dividend reinvestment service (not restricted to the dividend of a specific investment trust) and facility for making small occasional purchase of investment trust shares either for self or as gift.

Suitable for: Regular modest savings topped up by occasional lump sum investment. A cheaper-than-average way into the stock market.

Open to: Anyone.

Min–Max: £20–£25 a month, £250 occasional lump sum. No maximum.

Charges: Trust managers able to negotiate much lower stockbroker buying charges, usually between 0–0.2 per cent, for block purchase of trust shares. 50p per transaction.

Withdrawals: Sell shares through a stockbroker at current market prices, and, in the majority of cases, at normal stockbroker fees, although managers increasingly able to offer a special dealing rate on disposals too. You will receive your money in two to three weeks.

Interest: Variable, called "dividend" and usually paid half-yearly either by cheque or direct to bank account.

Tax: Interest is paid net of basic rate tax, the amount deducted known as "tax credit" can be reclaimed by non-taxpayers; higher rate taxpayers must pay more. Although investment trust itself is not liable to capital gains tax, gains made by investment trust company shareholders are liable to capital gains tax.

Children: Shares bought for a child must be registered in adult's name.

How to invest: Apply to investment trust secretary or manager of group.

Record: Share certificate.

Money Mail Rating: ***!! to *!!!!

Investor protection: Most management companies to belong to IMRO, Investment Management Regulatory Organisation and investors are covered by its compensation scheme, maximum £48,000.

Comment: The number of investment trusts and management seeking to expand their market with savings schemes is growing. Over half AITC's

223 members are included in savings schemes: some of the best known are run by Alliance, Baillie Gifford, Dunedin, Fleming, Foreign & Colonial, Ivory & Sime and Touche Remnant. Twenty groups are now offering an investment trust PEP on a regular savings basis.

Ordinary Quoted

Lump sum investment in shares "quoted" on the Stock Exchange. To achieve that status, the company must have been thoroughly vetted by the Stock Exchange to make sure it is well managed and financially sound; this includes a five year track record and at least 25 per cent of its share capital sold at the time the company came to the market as a new issue. The investor's objectives are rising dividend income, and a rising share price. But shares can fall in value too, and companies have failed.

Suitable for: Long term build-up of capital; short term speculation. Although you hope to make a profit out of share investment, remember it is a risk investment. Shareholders' perks, where available, are a bonus not a reason for buying.

Open to: Anyone.

Min–Max: Theoretically, one share in a company can be bought. In practice £400–£500 per shareholding is more realistic, and several shareholdings desirable.

Charges: Stockbrokers' fees no longer fixed. Most common commission for deals under £7,000–£8,000 is 1.5–1.65 per cent with minimum fee of £20–£25. Lower fees for larger transactions. Commission is not charged on new issues. Most banks are building up sophisticated share dealing services.

Withdrawals: In any amount, at current market price with money back after two to three weeks.

Interest: Variable, with dividend paid half-yearly by cheque or direct to bank account. When shares go ex-dividend, about five weeks before dividend date, the seller not the buyer receives the next dividend should the shares be sold in that period.

Tax: Dividends are paid net of basic rate tax, the amount deducted known as "tax credit" can be reclaimed by non-taxpayers; higher rate taxpayers pay more. Gains made by shareholder liable to capital gains tax.

Children: Shares bought for a child must be registered in adult's name.

How to invest: The Stock Exchange will provide names of firms willing to take on new clients; but limited advice given unless a) you are an advisory client and charged more, or b) a discretionary client where the broker manages your portfolio without consulting you first (although you will be informed). Most banks now strengthening their sharedealing services and High Street share shops (provided backed by well-known firms) another option. Read City pages and investment magazines for up-to-date information and advice.

Record: Share certificate.

Money Mail Rating: ****! to !!!!!

Investor protection: Share selling covered by the Financial Services Act, and investors covered by compensation scheme of up to £48,000. This does not provide protection against poor shareholdings but unscrupulous selling of shares.

Comment: Share investment is fun and rewarding provided you accept the risk that shares can fall in value, and are also prepared to work at your investments by keeping tabs on share prices and events which might affect your shareholding. Otherwise buy unit trusts or investment trusts and let the managers do the work for you. Preference shares, a fixed interest share investment where the shares rise or fall, rarely recommended.

Personal Equity Plan

Lump sum or regular savings up to a set limit of £6,000 each year invested in UK shares, companies on the Unlisted Securities Market, unit trusts and investment trusts. (Now shares quoted in the EC are counted as suitable investments for a PEP.) Registered PEP managers, often banks, unit trust groups and stockbrokers, offer investors a choice ranging from one to 10 shares, individual share selection, a mixture of units and shares. Unit trust and investment trusts now qualify for the full £6,000 investment. Rules have been relaxed so that PEPs no longer need to be held for a full calendar year to qualify for tax concessions and dividend income can be paid tax free to the PEP holder (not just reinvested). Switching between shares, tax free, is allowed. In addition investors are able to invest £3,000 into a single-company PEP in addition to their main PEP.

Suitable for: Long term build-up of tax-free capital; school fee planning, retirement planning; higher rate taxpayers.

Open to: Anyone 18 or over who does not have a current year PEP.

Min–Max: Varies: £25–£30 a month, £250 lump sum minimum; £500 a month, £6,000 lump sum maximum.

Charges: Initial fee 1–5 per cent, or £30–£70; annual fees 1–2 per cent. Additional charges of £20–£35 to attend shareholders' meetings.

Withdrawals: At any time and at current market value.

Interest: Variable.

Tax: Proceeds are free of capital gains tax and dividend income is tax free.

Children: No.

How to invest: Offered mainly by banks and unit trust groups. Comprehensive list of PEP managers, their addresses and investment range and charges of their PEPs published in the *PEP Investor*. *PEP guide* lists investment strategy and charges. You need to know your National Insurance number.

Record: Certificate.

Money Mail Rating: ***!! to **!!!

Investor protection: The Financial Services Act covers PEPs, and investors covered by compensation scheme of up to £48,000.

Comment: Capital gains tax does not

affect many investors, so this particular tax concession only becomes valuable over the long term when other PEPs have been taken out, but it is a flexible form of regular savings compared with life assurance savings and likely to become increasingly popular, for example, for school fees planning, and linked to a mortgage instead of an endowment policy. Check the charges, particularly the level of annual fees and the dealing cost of shares.

Permanent Interest Bearing Shares

Permanent interest bearing shares are quoted and traded on the London Stock Exchange. They are issued by building societies and pay an above-average fixed rate of interest but the value of your capital will go up and down with the price. The shares are irredeemable which means the society does not have to repay the principal. The only way you can get your capital back is to sell the shares. How much you get back depends on the market price of the shares, which can go up and down with demand.

Suitable for: Large investors looking to increase income as part of a portfolio. They are not suitable for savers looking for the best return on their High Street savings.

Open to: Anyone.

Min–Max: £1,000; no maximum.

Charges: You pay commission to stockbrokers on buying and selling. Cost is usually 0.5–0.75 per cent, depending on the size of the deal.

Withdrawals: On demand by selling the shares. The proceeds depends on the price at the time of selling.

Interest: Paid out half-yearly. Interest payments are non-cumulative so if the society fails to make a payout, it is under no obligation to make the payment at a future date.

Tax: Interest is paid net of basic rate tax which can be reclaimed by non-taxpayers. If you sell the shares at a profit, there is no capital gains tax to pay.

Children: Not suitable.

How to invest: Through a stockbroker.

Record: Share certificate.

Money Mail Rating: **!!!

Investor protection: PIBS are not covered by the building society savings compensation fund. PIBS holders are last in line for a payout if the society is wound up or dissolved.

Comment: PIBS are a new type of share issued by building societies. They offer a high fixed interest but, unlike all other building society investments, your capital is at risk. Unlike ordinary gilt-edged securities, PIBS do not have a redemption date when you get your capital back – as a result their market price is extremely sensitive to the level of interest rates. Initially these shares were aimed at huge investors but recent issues allow for a minimum purchase of £1,000. Building societies which so far offer PIBS with a low initial investment include Bradford & Bingley (minimum £10,000), and Bristol & West, Britannia, Leeds & Holbeck and Skipton, all with a minimum of £1,000.

Shares quoted on the Unlisted Securities Market

Lump sum investment in the Stock Exchange's junior market, the Unlisted Securities Market (USM). Unlike shares which are listed on the Stock Exchange, companies coming to the USM do not have to be as large, as well-established or release as large a proportion of their shares to the public. With USM companies the minimum trading period is two years and 10 per cent of the capital must be offered. Dividends are sometimes paid, but the object is to invest for capital gain not income. USM shares can be included in Personal Equity Plan portfolios, and many have moved up to a full listing on the Stock Exchange.

Suitable for: Investors who wish to build up a long term stake in new companies; higher rate taxpayers actively avoiding income. Not suitable for "widows and orphans". Investors who, if needs be, can afford to lose their money.

Open to: Anyone.

Min–Max: Realistic minimum £500; no maximum but with fewer shares available, it is sometimes difficult to buy large amounts.

Charges: Stockbroker fees of 1.5–1.65 per cent.

Withdrawals: At market price; there will be a larger spread between the buying and selling prices.

Interest: Variable, paid net of basic rate tax, and usually low.

Tax: Higher rate taxpayers must pay more on dividends; non-taxpayers can reclaim basic rate tax deducted; profits liable to capital gains tax.

Children: Not suitable.

How to invest: Through a stockbroker, but ask his advice; check financial pages for press comment about forthcoming newcomers to the USM.

Record: Share certificate.

Money Mail Rating: **!!! to !!!!!

Investor protection: The Securities Association's compensation fund, maximum £48,000 is now in force.

Comment: The casualty rate of USM companies is not high, but their investment performance has been mixed; the Third Market for even smaller companies only opened at the beginning of 1987 and was closed on 1 January 1991. Consider Business Expansion Schemes as a long term alternative. Never buy unquoted shares in foreign companies, and never buy shares from any organisation outside the UK.

Unit Trust

An investment collective: individual unitholders pool their money which is professionally managed and invested in a wide spread of share and sometimes Government stocks. Unit trust prices mirror the value of the underlying portfolio, and like all equity investments can rise or fall in value. Investors have a choice of investing for income, capital growth or a mixture of both; investing broadly based general funds covering the entire market spectrum either in the UK or overseas, or combining both, or in specialist funds which concentrate on one country or commercial activity. Later in 1991, unit trusts will be available in a wider range of investments including futures and options, warrants and real property.

Suitable for: First time investors in shares; investors wanting to concentrate on one specific overseas investment area; long term savings for children; investors prepared to sacrifice high immediate income in favour of rising income.

Open to: Anyone.

Min–Max: Commonly £500, sometimes £1,000 minimum. No maximum.

Charges: Initial charge of 3¼–5 per cent built into the "spread", the difference between the buying and selling price units which is generally 6–7 per cent. Annual fee of ½–1½ per cent taken out of the fund's income.

Withdrawals: Managers have to buy back your units and you will receive the current market buying or "bid" price (the lower of the two quoted) with some groups. The quoted price will no longer be the one dealt at as new rules permit managers to offer "forward pricing" which means that like investment in shares, you do not exactly know the price until after the deal is concluded; partial withdrawals if sufficient minimum balance retained. Sell by telephone, endorse your unit certificate and return to manager. You will receive your money about a week later.

Interest: Variable, called "distribution" and either paid twice yearly or automatically reinvested if the units are "accumulation" units. A few groups offer monthly income based on a set of unit trusts with different distribution dates.

Tax: Interest is paid net of basic rate tax, the amount deducted known as a "tax credit" can be reclaimed by non-taxpayers; higher rate taxpayers pay more. Although unit trust itself is not liable to capital gains tax, gains made by unitholders are liable to capital gains tax.

Children: Units can be held on behalf of a child and are "designated" with the child's name or initials.

How to invest: At the beginning of April 1991 there were 161 unit trust management companies running 1,409 unit trusts. Most of these are listed in the national press with address and telephone number. Managers will send details about any fund. You can buy and sell by phone.

Record: A contract note itemising your purchase is followed by a certificate once you have paid for the units.

Money Mail Rating: ****! to *!!!!

Investor protection: Unitholders' assets are actually held on their behalf by a trustee, usually a major bank or insurance company, formerly approved by the Government but now under the Investment Management Regulatory Organisation (IMRO). In addition each unit trust is authorised by Securities and Investments Board (SIB). The appropriate compensation scheme provides cover up to a maximum of £48,000.

Comment: There is a wide variation in investment performance. Unless you are actively prepared to manage your unit trust investments, go first for the broadly based unit trust which you can forget about for years. Specialist funds need careful monitoring: last year's winner is frequently this year's laggard. New unit trusts are often offered at a small discount and tend to perform well initially. Study unit trust "form" in magazine and newspaper articles. Watch charges: groups such as Murray Johnstone and Gartmore are spearheading a move to bring down or eliminate initial charges. *Money Management* and *Planned Savings* magazines publish comprehensive performance tables.

Unit Trust or Investment Trust PEP

Modest lump sum or regular savings investment into a personal equity plan invested exclusively in either unit or investment trusts limited to a maximum of £3,000 a year. The proceeds and dividend income are tax free.

Suitable for: First time investors; regular savings; higher rate taxpayers in particular.

Open to: Anyone aged 18 or over who does not already have a current year PEP.

Min–Max: £25–£50 minimum. Lump sum minimum usually £1,000 but can be lower; maximum £3,000. Or £900 if you invest in a fund which has less than 50 per cent of its holdings in UK shares at the moment, EC shares (including the UK) since 1991.

Charges: Vary. Sometimes normal unit trust charges; others have PEP initial fee of 1–5 per cent and waive or reduce unit trust charges. Additional charges of £20–£25 to attend shareholders' meetings.

Withdrawals: At any time and at current market value; partial withdrawals may be permitted.

Interest: Variable.

Tax: The proceeds are free of capital gains tax and interest is tax free.

Children: No.

How to invest: Phone or write to unit trust and investment trust management groups for details. Compare charges in specialist publications such as *PEP Investor* or *PEP guide*. You need to know your National Insurance number.

Record: Certificate.

Money Mail Rating: ***!! to **!!!

Investor protection: The Financial Services Act includes PEPs, and investors are covered by compensation scheme of up to £48,000.

Comment: Check that there is little or no element of double charging in respect of PEP and unit trust fees; do not take out a unit trust or investment trust PEP if you want to increase your PEP holding in the current year as investors are only permitted one a year.

Remember, you will need to know your National Insurance number when applying for any PEP. Husbands and wives cannot jointly own a PEP, but each can individually take one out.

Unit Trust Savings Scheme

Regular savings scheme for unlimited period into a unit trust, see page 97. Flexible: additional savings can be made at any time; savings can be stopped at any time, and either sold in part or together, or held as a lump sum investment. Minimum monthly savings can be very small.

Suitable for: Savers who cannot afford the minimum lump sum investment in unit trusts; regular savers building up capital from income.

Open to: Anyone.

Min–Max: Commonly £25–£30, sometimes £50 a month. No maximum.

Charges: Initial charge of 3¼–5 per cent built into the "spread", the difference of 6–7 per cent between the buying and selling price units. Annual fee of ½–1½ per cent taken out of the fund's income.

Withdrawals: Managers have to buy back your units and you will receive the current market buying or "bid" price. Partial withdrawals sometimes allowed. You will receive your money about a week later

Interest: Variable, and either accumulated within the units or used to buy extra units.

Tax: Interest is paid net of basic rate tax, the amount deducted known as "tax credit" can be reclaimed by non-taxpayers; higher rate taxpayers must pay more. Unitholders are liable to capital gains tax.

Children: Units can be held on behalf of a child and are designated with child's name or initials.

How to invest: Most of the major unit trust groups run a monthly savings plan; newer groups formed by insurance companies and most of the stockbroker unit trust groups might not have a regular savings plan. Ask managers for application form.

Record: Half-yearly statement of interest and the number of units bought each period sent.

Money Mail Rating: ****! to *!!!!

Investor protection: Unitholders' assets are actually held on their behalf by a trustee, usually a major bank or insurance company; formerly approved by the Government but now under IMRO, the Investment Management Regulatory Organisation. In addition each unit trust is authorised by SIB, Securities and Investments Board which has a compensation scheme providing cover of up to a maximum of £48,000.

Comment: Regular purchases of units

helps to iron out fluctuations in unit prices. Investors who believe in investment cycles should use a savings scheme to buy plenty of units in a specialist fund while the price is low at the bottom of the cycle. Otherwise stick to a general fund for a longer term investment. Almost certainly cheaper, initially, than a monthly savings plan into a unit trust PEP although over the long term, the PEP will probably be the more rewarding investment.

Government Index-Linked

Government index-linked stock are identical to fixed interest Government stock except in two very important respects. Instead of paying a fixed rate of interest, a modest fixed rate of interest is increased over each six month period in line with increases in the Retail Price Index. At the end of the stock's fixed life span, the nominal value repaid is also increased in line with increases in the Retail Price Index since its issue.

Suitable for: Anyone wishing to protect their capital from inflation; for higher rate taxpayers, the yields are not high and the stocks are bought for capital appreciation.

Open to: Anyone.

Min–Max: See Government Stock.

Charges: See Government Stock.

Withdrawals: Any amount at current market price which will not mirror, at this stage, changes in the Retail Price Index; at redemption when price will reflect increase in Retail Price Index since the stock was issued.

Interest: Variable, and will reflect changes in the Retail Price Index over a six month period. See Government Stock for "ex-dividend".

Tax: See Government Stock.

Children: See Government Stock.

How to invest: See Government Stock.

Record: Stock certificate.

Money Mail Rating: ***** if held to redemption, otherwise ****!

Investor protection: Guaranteed by Government; The Securities Association compensation scheme provides cover up to a maximum of £48,000.

Comment: In periods of relatively low inflation these stocks have not performed as well as conventional fixed interest stock, but are likely to improve their rating if inflation rises. National Savings index-linked certificates could be a better medium to short term investment although maximum investment is limited.

Index-Linked Stock

	(a)
2% Treasury 1996	267.9
2½% Treasury 2001	308.8
2½% Treasury 2003	310.7
2% Treasury 2006	274.1
2½% Treasury 2009	310.7
2½% Treasury 2011	294.1
2½% Treasury 2013	351.9
2½% Treasury 2016	322.0
2½% Treasury 2020	327.3
2½% Treasury 2024	385.3

(a) ***RPI base month for index-linking. (Index rebased Jan 1987=100. Divide old figure by 3.945)***

Government Stock

(commonly called Gilt-Edged Securities)

Lump sum investment in a stock issued by the Government as part of its fund-raising programme. Most stocks are issued with a fixed interest rate and a fixed life span, at the end of which the Government will redeem them in full, at the "nominal" value.

The yield, the return the investor gets from stock at that price, is the yardstick for investing in gilts. If interest rates in general fall, higher-yielding stock will be in demand and the stock price rise, ultimately driving the yield down; conversely if interest rates are rising, investors will sell their gilts (to get a better return elsewhere) and the price of the stock will fall forcing the yield up. When you see gilts quoted in the press, you will often see two yields: one is the straight interest/price yields, the other, the "net redemption" yield takes into account the capital gain or loss, averaged out, you would make if the stock were held to redemption.

Suitable for: Most taxpayers, who should buy stocks appropriate to their tax bracket; higher rate taxpayers will be more interested in capital gains while the high yield on others makes them a suitable investment for a retirement portfolio.

Open to: Anyone.

Min–Max: Theoretically no minimum, but £250–£500 more practical in view of the commission to be paid. No maximum, except for stock bought from the National Savings Stock Register where the maximum daily purchase of any one stock is £10,000.

Charges: On gilts bought from the National Savings Stock Register (via your local post office), the charges are £1 including VAT for purchases of £250 and below, and £1 plus 50p for every additional £125 (or part); on sales the fees including VAT are 10p for every £10 (or part) for deals of less than £100, between £100–£250 £1, over £250, £1 and further 50p for every additional £125 (or part). This works out at 0.4 per cent. The charges for buying gilts through a stockbroker or bank vary, ranging from 0.4 per cent up to £20,000 to 1.5 per cent up to £5,000. Shop around. There are no charges if you buy a new issue or when the stock is redeemed.

Withdrawals: Any amount at the current market price; or at redemption date.

Interest: Fixed, paid half-yearly, net of basic rate tax if bought through a stockbroker or bank, except for War Loan where dividends are always without deduction of tax. If bought from the National Savings Stock Register, dividends are paid gross. Stocks go ex-dividend about five weeks before the dividend date, with the interest going to the seller not the buyer. This is reflected in the price as the interest due to the next dividend date is subtracted from the stock price.

Tax: Investors are liable to tax on the gross dividend payment from stock on the National Savings Stock Register; higher rate taxpayers must pay more on dividends from stock bought through a stockbroker or bank where basic rate tax is deducted at source; non-taxpayers can reclaim the tax. Gilts are exempt from capital gains tax.

Stock on National Savings Stock Register

Description of stock	Interest payable on	
10% Treasury 1992	**21 Feb**	21 Aug
12¼% Exchequer 1992	25 Feb	**25 Aug**
13½% Exchequer 1992	22 Mar	**22 Sept**
6% Funding 1993	15 Mar	**15 Sept**
13¾% Treasury 1993	23 May	**23 Nov**
14½% Treasury 1994	**1 Mar**	1 Sept
9% Treasury 1994	17 May	**17 Nov**
12% Treasury 1995	**25 Jan**	25 Jul
12¾% Treasury 1995	15 May	**15 Nov**
9% Treasury 1992–96	**15 Mar**	15 Sept
15¼% Treasury 1996	**3 May**	3 Nov
13¼% Exchequer 1996	**15 May**	15 Nov
2% Index-linked 1996	16 Mar	**16 Sept**
3% Redemption 1986–96	1 Apr	**1 Oct**
13¼% Treasury 1997	**22 Jan**	22 Jul
8¾% Treasury 1997	1 Mar	**1 Sept**
6¾% Treasury 1995–98	**1 May**	1 Nov
15½% Treasury 1998	30 Mar	**30 Sept**
9½% Treasury 1999	**15 Jan**	15 Jul
12¼% Exchequer 1999	**26 Mar**	26 Sept
9% Conversion 2000	**3 Mar**	3 Sept
13% Treasury 2000	14 Jan	**14 Jul**
14% Treasury 1998–2001	**22 May**	22 Nov
13¾% Treasury 2000–03	25 Jan	**25 Jul**
3½% Funding 1999–2004	14 Jan	**14 Jul**
12½% Treasury 2003–05	21 May	**21 Nov**
2% Index-linked 2006	19 Jan	**19 Jul**
8% Treasury 2002–06	5 Apr	**5 Oct**
2½% Index-linked 2011	23 Feb	**23 Aug**
5½% Treasury 2008–12	10 Mar	**10 Sept**
7¾% Treasury 2012–15	**26 Jan**	26 Jul
2½% Index-linked 2016	26 Jan	**26 Jul**
2½% Index-linked 2020	**16 Apr**	16 Oct
2½% Index-linked 2024	17 Jan	**17 Jul**
4% Consols	1 Feb	1 Aug
3½% War	1 Jun	1 Dec
3½% Conversion	1 Apr	1 Oct
2½% Treasury 1975 or after	1 Apr	1 Oct
2½% Consols 2½% Annuities 2¾% Annuities	5 Jan 5 Jul	5 Apr 5 Oct

Redemption month in bold

Children: Stock brought through stockbrokers or bank must be in an adult's name; stock from the National Savings Stock Register can be in the child's name. Children's holdings cannot be transferred to the Bank of England's Stock Register until they are 18.

How to invest: Through a stockbroker or bank for stock held on the Bank of England Stock Register – this is a comprehensive list. About 50 representative stocks are held on the National Savings Stock Register for which application forms for purchase are available at your post office. The form is DNS 400 (GS1); repurchase forms and envelopes are also available at the post office.

Record: Stock certificate.

Money Mail Rating: ***** if held to redemption, otherwise ****!

Investor protection: Guaranteed by the Government; The Securities Association compensation scheme, providing up to £48,000, is now in force.

Comment: Dealing through a stockbroker or bank will give you a more immediate price; you might get the next or an even later day's price on purchases from the National Savings Stock Register. But the dealing costs are cheaper and interest is paid without deduction of tax. It is possible to switch from one register to another: obtain the forms from either the Bank of England or Bonds and Stock Office, Blackpool FY3 9YP.

Loan and Debenture

Lump sum investment in a stock issued by a company at a fixed rate of interest over a fixed period. At the end of the period, the stock is redeemed in full, but until that point is dealt in at market prices which can rise or fall. As with Government fixed rate stock, company stock is quoted with a net redemption yield, reflecting any capital gains or losses to be made from that point until maturity, as well as the interest return. Some loan stocks are convertible into ordinary shares at fixed date and price.

Suitable for: Most taxpayers whether they want income or capital growth.

Open to: Anyone aged 18 or over.

Min–Max: Realistic minimum £1,000–£2,000; no maximum.

Charges: Stockbroker's typical commission 0.9 per cent on first £5,000, 0.45 per cent on next £5,000, less on larger amounts. No fees on new issues nor on redemption.

Withdrawals: Any amount at market value; or at redemption date.

Interest: Fixed, paid half-yearly with basic rate tax deducted. Stock goes ex-dividend about five weeks before interest is paid which means the seller, not buyer, keeps the interest, although the price is adjusted downwards accordingly.

Tax: Higher rate taxpayers must pay more, non-taxpayers can reclaim tax deducted. Stocks exempt from capital gains tax.

Children: In adult's name.

How to invest: Through a stockbroker or bank; check convertible options, redemption dates and long term outlook for the company before proceeding.

Record: Stock certificate.

Money Mail Rating: ***** if held to redemption, otherwise ****! to ***!!

Investor protection: If a company fails, debenture holders have a prior claim to be paid in full ahead of other creditors. The Securities Association's compensation scheme, maximum compensation £48,000, is now in force.

Comment: Stick to well-known companies; the convertible option can be an attractive way of building up an equity portfolio later.

APPENDIX ONE

Shareholder perks

Many companies give perks to shareholders based on the number of shares owned. Some are more attractive and worthwhile than others; but none should be considered as the reason for buying the shares in the first place. Treat the perk as a welcome bonus instead.

The following list, detailing perks by type, and then itemising the individual companies and minimum shareholding to qualify, is based on information supplied by stockbrokers Kleinwort Benson, last updated in 1988. Benefits may be altered or withdrawn at any time.

Books
Pentos (*Dillions, University, Hudsons etc. Bookshops*)
Alfred Preedy & Sons

Camping Equipment
Peters Stores

Carpets
Cattles
E. Upton & Sons

China & Glassware
Asprey
Boots
Alfred Preedy & Sons
Toye & Co.
E. Upton

Clocks & Watches
Asprey
Boots
Ciro
Fobel International
London & Midland Industries
Toye & Co.

Clothing & Fashion Wear
Alexon Group
N. Brown Investments (*woollens*)
Burton Group
Cattles
Dunlop
Cecil Gee
Gieves Group (*Gieves & Hawkes*)
Greenfields Leisure
Laura Ashley
Moss Bros.
Next
Peters Stores
Austin Reed

Clothing Hire
Moss Bros.

Confectionery
Boots
Alfred Preedy & Sons

Department Stores
Bentalls
Boots
Cattles
Hillards
E. Upton

Double Glazing
London & Northern Group (*Weatherseal*)

Dry Cleaning
Johnson Group
Sketchley

Electrical
Boots
Cattles
Fobel International
Securicor Group

Entertainment
All England Tennis (*Centre Court seats*)
Ferguson Ind. Holdings
Greyhound Racing Association (*GRA Stadiums*)
Kursaal
Ladbroke Group
Trusthouse Forte (*Talk of the Town*)

Finance & Investments
Britannia Arrow
Fredericks Place Group

Food
Associated British Foods
Boots
Park Food Group
Ranks Hovis McDougall

Furniture
A. Arenson (*Arvin*)
British Vita
Cattles
Courts (*Furnishers*)
London & Midland Industrials
E. Upton
World of Leather

Gardening
Boots
Cramphorn
Sharpe & Fisher
William Sinclair

Holidays
Allied-Lyons
Barclays Unicorn Group
Barr & Wallace Arnold Trust
Bass (*Pontinental*)
Cattles
Henlys
Ladbroke Group
Lonrho
Mount Charlotte Invs.
Prince of Wales Hotels
Rank Organisation
Stakis
Trafalgar House (*Cunard*)
Trusthouse Forte (*Swan Hellenic*)

Hotel
Allied-Lyons
Barr & Wallace Arnold Trust
Bass (*Crest*)
Eurotunnel
Goldsmiths Groups
Greenall Whitley
Kennedy Brookes
Ladbroke Group
Lonrho
Mount Charlotte Investments
Norfolk Capital Group
Prince of Wales Hotels
Queens Moat Houses
Rank Organisation
Securicor Group
Stakis
Scottish & Newcastle Breweries (*Thistle*)
Trafalgar House (*Ritz*)

APPENDIX ONE

Trusthouse Forte
Vaux Breweries

Household Equipment
Bellway
Boots
British Vita
Cattles
Emess Lighting
Fobel International (*telephones*)
Kalon
London & Midland Industrials (*home extensions*)
Lonrho (*Brentfords*)
Manders
Mellarware Int'l
Yale & Valor

Houses
Barratt Developments
Bellway

Jewellery
Asprey
Goldsmiths Group
Ratners
Toye

Motor Vehicles
Alexander Holdings (*Ford*)
Barr & Wallace Arnold Trust (*Vauxhall, Volkswagen, Audi, Opel, Cadillac & Ford*)
Lonrho (*Volkswagen, Audi*)

Motorists' Tools
BSG Int'l
Spear & Jackson Int.

Paint/Wallpaper
Manders Holdings
Norcros
Sharpe & Fisher
E. Upton

Regalia
Toye & Co.

Restaurants
Associated Leisure
Bentalls
Eurotunnel
Grand Metropolitan
Imperial Group
Kennedy Brookes
Ladbroke Group
Scottish & Newcastle Breweries
Stakis
Trusthouse Forte
Vaux Breweries
Whitbread

Shoes
Gieves Group
Moss Bros.
Austin Reed
Stylo.

Silverware
Asprey
Toye & Co.

Sporting Goods
Peters Stores
Alfred Preedy & Sons
Riley Leisure
Trusthouse Forte (*Lillywhites*)

Stationery
Alfred Preedy & Sons

Toys & Games
Boots
Fobel International
Alfred Preedy & Sons
Riley Leisure

Travel
Eurotunnel
Peninsular & Oriental Steam Navigation Company

Tyres
Kwik-Fit (*Tyres & Exhausts*)

Wines & Spirits
Allied-Lyons
Fuller-Smith Turner
Grand Metropolitan (*Justerini & Brooks*)
Greene King
Merrydown Wine Co.
Mt. Charlotte Investments (*Bronte*)
Whitbread (*Thresher*)

Miscellaneous
Abbey Life
Britannia Arrow
Berry Birch Noble
C.G.A.
Dominion International Group

LIST OF COMPANIES PROVIDING BENEFITS FOR SHAREHOLDERS

Company	Brief details of benefits	Minimum shareholding to qualify
Abbey Life	Occasional offers to unit holders on products and services.	100 Ordinary shares.
Alexanders Holdings	Discount of around 2% on new vehicles at dealerships listed below: Alexanders of Edinburgh Ltd Alexanders of Kirkintilloch Ltd Alexanders of Greenock Ltd Alexanders of Northampton Ltd	2,000 Ordinary shares.
Alexon Group	15% discount on Alexon goods. Shareholder card issued.	1,000 Ordinary shares.
All England Tennis (Stock tightly held and not generally marketable.) Cost of two Debentures for 1986/90 series in excess of £8,000.	1 free Centre Court ticket per day for every 1 £50 Debenture held. (Minimum purchase is two Debentures.) Entry to Lounge and Buffet Bar at Centre Court, and reserved car parking space adjacent to the Centre Court (for a small fee). Priority for 1991/95 series.	2 £50 (nominal) non-interest bearing Wimbledon Debentures.

APPENDIX ONE

Allied-Lyons	10% discount on Embassy Hotel Breaks. Periodical wine offers and discount vouchers on Victoria Wine purchases. Discount vouchers for use in certain restaurants.	No minimum.
Arenson Group	15% on "Arvin" domestic furniture and "Roomsets" bedroom furniture.	Ordinary and Preference shares – no minimum. Unit trusts and investment trusts with holdings may nominate beneficiary.
Asprey	Asprey card, sent when holding registered, giving 15% discount on most cash purchases from Aspreys in Bond Street and 153 Fenchurch Street.	1,125 Ordinary shares.
Associated British Foods	Gift of some of the company's product (approximately 8 grocery items), at AGM. Worth approximately £5–£6.	No minimum.
BSG International	Special terms on car purchases, leasing and servicing. 50% discount on all Britax seat-belts and child safety equipment.	No minimum.
Barclays Unicorn Group	Special rates on a number of Cunard cruise holidays are available to investors.	All unit holders.
Barr and Wallace Arnold	7½% discount on package holidays, 5% discount on accommodation at Oswalds Hotel, Torquay. 10% discount on a new car, without trade-in, at any of the group's garages.	250 Ordinary or "A" shares.
Barratt Developments	Discount on purchase of new house. £500 per £25,000 or part thereof of the purchase of a Barratt property. Thus a shareholder purchasing a property for £30,000 would be entitled to a discount of £1,000.	1,000 Ordinary shares held at least 12 months.
Bass	Shareholder benefit card entitles holder to 15% discount off full tariff price at all Crest Hotels Monday to Thursday. On Fri, Sat, Sun and public holidays most Crest Hotels offer "Two for the price of one" charging only the normal single price for a double or twin room. Holders are entitled to 15% off this rate, which is based on a 1–3 night stay exclusive of meals. Holders also enjoy 15% off all Crest Welcome Breaks. Prices for bed and breakfast only are available in London, Amsterdam and other Crest Hotels on the continent. 10% reduction in the cost of a Pontins UK holiday subject to availability for the shareholder up to a maximum of four persons.	Ordinary shares – 50 shares OR Preference shares – 50.
Bellway	£500–£2,500 discount on price of a new Bellway house. 10% discount on Nixon Kitchen units.	1,000 Ordinary shares held for 1 year.
Bentalls	Discount vouchers entitling shareholder to total discounts of £25. Despatched with annual report.	100 Ordinary shares.
Berry Birch & Noble	10% discount on household insurance policies.	500 Ordinary shares.

APPENDIX ONE

Boots	10 £1 vouchers to be used towards a purchase of goods to the value of £5 per voucher. NOT valid for purchases of books or medicine.	100 Ordinary shares.
Britannia Arrow Holdings	2% discount at all times on an investment in any of the group's unit trusts.	1,000 Ordinary shares on register for 12 months.
British Vita	Discount of 15–35% on pillows, quilts, beds and sofa beds.	No minimum.
N. Brown Investments	20% discount on various items purchased from J.D. Williams and other mail order catalogues of the group. 20% discount on fashion wear of the group's Heather Valley (Woollens) subsidiary. Maximum discount allowable is £200.	No minimum.
Burton Group	12½% discount at Burton, Top Shop, Evans, D. Perkins, Top Man, Principles, Peter Robinson, Debenhams, Collier, Hamleys and Harvey Nichols. Shareholder card issued, giving credit limit of £5,000 (i.e. a discount of £625 in any year).	300 Ordinary shares.
Cattles	10% discount on Rosebys curtains & household textiles, 10% discount on Ewbanks mail order and discount warehouse, 5% discount on Shopachecks, valid in Burtons, Woolworths, Storehouse, Next etc. Special offers from Parkhill Travel. Shareholder card issued.	No minimum.
Courts Furnishers	10% discount on furniture.	100 Ordinary/"A" Ordinary on register for 3 months.
Cramphorn (USM)	10% discount on cash purchases excluding sale items at shops and garden centres. Discount card issued.	600 Ordinary shares held for 1 year.
Crown House	15% discount on certain products from the tableware division which includes Edinburgh Crystal, Thomas Webb Crystal and Denby Tableware available for the Group's shop-within-shops. Discount card issued.	250 Ordinary shares.
Dominion International Group	Shareholder Benefit Scheme, with right to participate in Annual Draw, held in the fourth quarter of each year. 6 shareholders then picked to visit a location of their choice in the UK or overseas wherever Dominion has business interests.	500 Ordinary shares held for at least 12 months prior to date of Draw.
Eldridge Pope	Discount on wines, beers, ciders and spirits. Details sent before Christmas.	No minimum.
Emess Lighting	30% discount on a range of light fittings.	100 Ordinary shares.
Eurotunnel	Discounts on travel, hotel rooms and restaurant meals.	Minimum 500 shares held since issue.
Ferguson Industrial Holdings	Free entry for up to 4 people to 12th century Appleby Castle (Co's registered office) on presentation of a copy of the annual report. The grounds are open to the public throughout the summer months.	No minimum.

APPENDIX ONE

Fobel International	Special offers on a variety of goods, covering TV games, teletext decoders, radio watches and view data printers, portable telephones and home computers.	No minimum.
Cecil Gee (USM)	Various discounts at Cecil Gee, Gee 2, Savoy Taylors Guild and Beale & Inman shops	
	One 10% discount voucher.	500 shares.
	Two 10% discount vouchers.	1,000 shares.
	A further discount voucher is sent out for each additional 1,000 shares held. (Vouchers may be used during sales.)	
	Discount vouchers are distributed once a shareholder has been on the register for 6 months.	
The Gieves Group	20% discount on goods purchased from branches of Gieves & Hawkes. Shareholder's Concession Card issued.	600 Ordinary shares held for 3 months.
Goldsmiths Group	15% off all jewellery at the retail shop outlets. 20% discount on accommodation and food at Heritage Hotels. 5% discount on services provided by Swinton/Gover insurance outlets.	No minimum.
GRA Group	Invitation to shareholder and 1 guest to spend an evening at one of the stadiums. 1 free voucher for car park also sent.	No minimum.
Grand Metropolitan Hotels	Voucher offering £4 off a meal for 2 at any Berni Inn. Various discounts on wine, mixed cases of wine & spirits, beer, lager, sherry, spirits and sports goods. 15% discount on spectacles or contact lenses from Pearle Vision centres in the UK.	No minimum
Greenall Whitley	10% discount on current G.W. or De Vere Hotel tariff.	No minimum.
	10% discount on G.W. or De Vere Hotels "Breakaway Weekend" rates.	400 Ordinary shares or 2,000 "A" Ordinary shares.
	10% discount on "Before you Fly Package".	
	Periodic. 10% discount on 1 summer and 1 winter holiday publicised in the current Arrowsmith or Skyfares brochures – flights from Manchester only.	
Greene King	Special offers on wine.	No minimum.
Hillards	Discount at Hillards stores during the Christmas period. 5 vouchers of £3 each off purchases exceeding £30. (Not on cigarettes or petrol.) Sent out with annual report and account. Shareholders attending AGM receive lunch.	200 Ordinary shares.
Johnson Group	12 vouchers each giving a £2.50 discount on orders of £10 or more. Each voucher valid for 1 month. Group trades under the Bollom, Crockett, Harris Harton Kreels, Pullars, Smiths & Zernys names.	No minimum. Coupons with annual report.
Kalon Group	Discount at Kalon DIY shops.	No minimum
Kennedy Brookes	20% discount at any of their restaurants. Including Maxims in London. Credit card issued.	500 Ordinary shares.

John Kent (USM)	10% discount on purchases from "John Kent" and "Smith" branches. Discount card issued upon registration and renewed with annual report.	500 Ordinary shares.
Kwik-Fit (Tyres & Exhausts) Holdings	10% discount on any purchase, worth £5 or more, from any of company's depots. Vouchers enclosed with report. Only 1 purchase per year.	100 Ordinary shares.
Ladbroke Group	10% discount on hotels, motor inns and holiday villages. 25% off accommodation rates at "Club In" Villa Resort, Eilat & LosZocos Lanzarote. Not available Christmas, New Year or Easter. 10% off restaurant meals & drinks at listed Astey Restaurants in Wales.	No minimum. (Ordinary, loan stock or warrants.)
Laura Ashley	10% discount voucher with annual report.	No minimum.
London & Midland Industrial	Discount of 10% on Compton Buildings, Banbury windows, Banbury Homes and Gardens and Falcon Pipe Group.	No minimum.
London and Northern Group	17½% discount on list prices of Weatherseal double glazing, patio doors, and replacement windows. Leaflet and form circulated to shareholders, or direct approach to Weatherseal.	250 Ordinary shares or 250 Preference. Employees of shareholding companies and institutions also eligible.
Lonrho	Periodical discount on Audi & Volkswagen motor cars. 25% discount on room rates in UK Metropole hotels. 10% discount on "Whileaway Holidays" at all UK hotels. 30% discount on full rate bedrooms at the Melville Hotel in Mauritius (valid for bookings through Kunoi Travel). Excluding November and December. 15% discount at Brentfords. £20 off a major service at a Dutton Forshaw garage. Special offer from Whyte & Mackay Distillers. Special offer from Southern Watch & Clock Supplies. 20% discount off room rates at Princess Hotels International. SEAT cars available to shareholders at special prices.	At company's discretion. 100 shares on register by 1 March.
LWT (Holdings)	10% discount on holidays with Page & Moy Ltd, Harborough Marine Ltd, Cresta World Travel Ltd and Sunspot Tours Ltd. Discount covers shareholder and family or friends travelling together on the same holiday.	No minimum.
Manders Holdings	Discount of 25% on brushes and sundries, 20% on paint and up to 30% on wallpaper. "Trade cash card" sent to shareholders.	No minimum.
Mellerware International	12% discount on Co's products (up to £250).	250 Ordinary shares.

APPENDIX ONE

Merrydown Wine (USM)	Approximately 20% discount on cases of wine and cider, inclusive of VAT. Shareholders invited to lunch and wine tasting after AGM.	50 Ordinary shares.
Moss Bros	10% discount on all goods and services, not at sale or special promotion prices. Discount card sent to holder. Second card sent to shareholder's spouse on request.	250 Ordinary shares held for 6 months.
Mount Charlotte Investments	10% discount on a "Value Break". 10% discount at all the Company's Hotels for Room and Breakfast. 15% discount on weekly terms for half board at the Company's 5 Family Holiday hotels. For terms other than half board the discount will be 10%. The discount does not apply to Self-Catering holidays. Holders may purchase Bronte Yorkshire Liqueur at special price. Shareholders Privilege card enclosed with proxy form.	1,000 Ordinary shares on register at the time of the announcement of the AGM.
Next	25% discount usable on one occasion only in any Next shop. Voucher issued with annual report, valid for 1 month.	500 Ordinary shares.
Norcros	10% discount on goods at UBM Building Supplies. Shareholder discount card issued.	No minimum.
Norfolk Capital Group	Vouchers issued with annual report and accounts entitling shareholders to a 20% discount at the Group's Hotels and restaurants. 10% discount on any Greatstay weekend booking and Norbreck Castle holiday package.	No minimum.
Park Food Group	20% discount on range of hampers.	No minimum.
Peninsular & Oriental Steam Navigation Company (P & O)	Aberdeen – Lerwick (Shetlands) . . . 30% discount on all sailings except July & August. Scrabster – Stromness (Orkney) . . . 30% discount. Restricted to 2 round trips in a 12 month period, return journeys only. Shareholder must travel. Shareholder qualifies as soon as his name is on the register. Caravans charged full fare.	200 Deferred shares. 500 Preferred shares.
	Subject to space availability, discount on the normal fare for the carriage of 1 private motor car (or motorised caravan or motorcycle) and 4 passengers (2 fare-paying children count as 1 passenger), including the shareholder, on an unlimited number of return journeys on qualifying routes and sailings, as follows: Dover to Calais, Boulogne, Zeebrugge, Ostend . . . 50% all sailings Felixstowe to Zeebrugge . . . 50% excluding "A" sailings Portsmouth to Cherbourg, Portsmouth to Le Havre . . . 40% excluding "A" sailings Cairnryan to Larne . . . 25% all sailings	£300 concessionary stock registered by 31 December in any year (half concessions).

	No single journey or open-date tickets. Applications specifying sailings and dates must be made by post at least 30 days before first date in July and August, otherwise 7 days, to the company's shareholders' Concessions Department. No concessions for caravans, sleeping accommodation or on-board catering. Payment for tickets can be made by credit cards but not by Eurocheques. *Please note that preference on bookings will be to full fare paying passengers.*	£600 concessionary stock registered by 31 December in any year (full concessions).
Pentos	Holders may apply for a discount card allowing 10% off any cash purchase at company's book shops and at Athena Galleries.	500 Ordinary or Deferred shares or a combination.
Peters Stores	15% discount on all cash purchases at any branch (general clothing, industrial and protective clothing, camping, sailing and sports equipment). Card with report in November. Buffet lunch for shareholders attending AGM.	No minimum.
Alfred Preedy & Sons	10% discount on purchases in excess of £3, at any of the group's 200 stores and shops, on all goods except cigarettes and tobacco, newspapers and magazines. (Goods include toys and games, books, records, artists' materials, china and glassware, sports equipment, confectionery, greeting cards.) Form with report.	250 Ordinary shares.
Prince of Wales Hotels	Vouchers despatched with annual report offering the following discounts:– 15% on B & B rates 15% on Budget Breakaway Holidays 15% on Restaurant bills plus introductory vouchers for friends' use offering the following discounts:– 10% on Restaurant bill 10% on Budget Breakaway Holidays	No minimum.
Queens Moat Houses	2 courtesy cheques for £4 towards food and drink when taking a meal in a Queens Moat House Hotel. One courtesy cheque worth £15 when taking Town and Country Classics weekend accommodation at a Queens Moat House Hotel.	No minimum.
Rank Organisation	**Holiday Scheme** 10% discount on brochure price of OSL, Wings, Ellerman Sunflight or Freshfields holidays up to a maximum holiday value of £5,000 for a shareholder and his party. Only 1 concession per booking. **Shareholder must travel.** **Hotels Scheme** 10% discount on normal published tariff at any Rank Hotel. 10% discount on special weekend rates available at certain times of the year.	500 Ordinary shares on register for at least 6 months at the date of departure or the holder of any number of Ordinary shares for a continuous period of 5 years up to date of departure.

APPENDIX ONE

Ranks Hovis McDougall	Hamper at AGM.	No minimum.
Ratners	Shareholders card issued each May giving 10% discount.	No minimum.
Austin Reed	15% discount but not on sale or special promotion prices	500 Ordinary or "A" Ordinary shares.
Riley Leisure	Approx. 20% discount on billiard tables and cues.	No minimum.
Scottish & Newcastle Breweries	£21 voucher for use at Thistle Hotels enclosed with report. Selection of wines offered at a discount.	No minimum.
Securicor Group	Periodical discounts on communications equipment and at Co's hotels in Coventry, Richmond and Ross-shire. Details with annual report.	No minimum.
Sharpe & Fisher	10% discount voucher for use in the Co's DIY supermarkets and Garden centres. Valid following account statement to 31 December.	No minimum.
Sketchley	25% discount on normal cost of dry cleaning and ancillary services. Discount card issued on registration and thereafter automatic annual renewal (on 1 August) as long as qualifying shareholding remains on register.	300 Ordinary or Preference shares.
Stakis	Vouchers despatched with annual report. 15% discount voucher on a Stakis summer holiday. £5 restaurant voucher. Voucher for £2 off 6 bottles of wine to the value of £15.	300 Ordinary shares.
Stylo	Vouchers giving 20% discount on 2 separate purchases of shoes, sent with report. Company sends copy of latest report to new holders, therefore double vouchers in first year.	No minimum.
Toye & Company	15% discount on purchases, from branches of Toye, Kenning & Spencer. (Civil and Military regalia, trophies, awards, medals, badges, jewellery, gold and silverware, cutlery, glassware, watches and clocks.) Does not apply to special offers or on postal orders. "Special purchase card" issued once name is entered on register.	250 Ordinary shares. Institutional holders not eligible.
Trafalgar House	10% discount on most QE2 and Sagafjord World Cruises. 15% discount on most other cruises. 15% discount at Cunard Hotels in UK and Caribbean.	250 Ordinary shares. Institutional and corporate holders may nominate one person to benefit.
Trusthouse Forte	10% discount on Leisure Gift Cheques for maximum £2,000 value. Application form enclosed with report. Can be used in settlement of accounts at THF Hotels, restaurants, and other THF establishments. GiFi cheques also exchangeable at Lillywhite stores for sports goods and clothing.	500 Ordinary.

E. Upton	15% discount on goods and services at company's stores excluding large electrical goods e.g. freezers, TVs, audio equipment where the discount is 10%. 10% discount on carpets where free fitting is offered.	250 Ordinary or "A" shares.
Vaux Breweries	"Swallowcard" for use in Swallow Hotels and Restaurants, Anchor Hotels and Taverns. 10% discount on accommodation and meals. Vouchers for use in Swallow Hotels providing discounted wines, Breakaway holidays, £25 off Leisure Club membership etc. Twice yearly wine offer. Buffet lunch at AGM.	No minimum.
Whitbread	Vouchers sent with annual report in June giving 10% discount on sales up to £300 in Beefeater Steakhouses, Roast Inns, Pizza Hut, Country Club Hotels, Coaching Inns, Thresher Off-Licenses.	No minimum.
William Sinclair (USM)	Order form sent with annual report giving first £5 of order free, 20% discount on the excess.	No minimum.
World of Leather (USM)	10% discount on leather furniture.	500 Ordinary shares held for minimum of 6 months.
Yale & Valor	Various products offered to shareholders at special prices throughout the year.	No minimum.
H. Young	Occasional wine offer.	No minimum.

APPENDIX TWO

Recent issues of National Savings Certificates

All the following issues are within the first five years of their life when fixed interest rates (pitched at a competitive level when the issue first goes on sale) apply. Thereafter variable interest is added every three months (see the general extension rate).

The compound rate of interest over the first five years is usually quoted. It is a useful yardstick for making long term (i.e. five years in this case) comparisons.

As interest payments are not constant but increase towards the end of the term, check both the annual yield and the average return obtained from holding from now until the end of the term for more immediate comparisons.

Once these certificates reach the end of the five year term variable interest is added every three months – known as the *general extension rate*. This is now below the compound rate of interest on the current issue of certificates and varies. The fixed interest rate extensions to older issues of certificates has been phased out and completely replaced by the general extension rate.

As interest is added either at three-monthly intervals (or four-monthly with older issues) when you cash in your certificates, do so immediately after a payment date. Check the purchase date on the certificates to calculate the interim anniversary dates.

Capital Bonds are not strictly speaking National Savings Certificates, because the interest is not tax free. It is accumulated before deduction of tax which has to be paid annually. However, their format is sufficiently similar to National Savings Certificates to include them in this detailed schedule of rates and values.

APPENDIX TWO

33rd Issue

Sold at £25 a unit from 1 May 1987 – 21 July 1988

Compound interest rate over 1st five years = 7%

Year	Interest: 3 monthly £	Value anniversary of purchase £	Yield anniversary of purchase %	Average yield to end term %
4	0.59½	32.16	8.0	8.5
5	0.72½	35.06	9.0	9.0

34th Issue

Sold at £25 a unit from 22 July 1988 – 16 June 1990

Compound interest rate over 1st five years = 7.5%

Year	Interest: 3 monthly £	Value anniversary of purchase £	Yield anniversary of purchase %	Average yield to end term %
2	0.43	28.22	6.5	7.9
3	0.49½	30.20	7.0	8.3
4	0.64½	32.77	8.5	9.0
5	0.78	35.89	9.5	9.5

35th Issue

Sold at £25 a unit from 18 June 1990 – 14 March 1991

Compound interest rate over 1st five years = 9.5%

Year	Interest: 3 monthly £	Value anniversary of purchase £	Yield anniversary of purchase %	Average yield to end term %
2	0.57¼	29.29	8.5	9.9
3	0.67¾	31.93	9.0	10.3
4	0.83¾	35.28	10.5	11.0
5	1.01½	39.35	11.5	11.5

APPENDIX TWO

36th Issue

Sold at £25 a unit from 2 April 1991

Compound interest rate over 1st five years = 8.5%

Year	Interest: 3 monthly £	Value anniversary of purchase £	Yield anniversary of purchase %	Average yield to end term %
1	1.75*	26.75	7.0	8.5
2	0.50	28.75	7.5	8.9
3	0.57½	31.05	8.0	9.3
4	0.73¾	34.00	9.5	10.0
5	0.89¼	37.59	10.5	10.5

* paid at end of first 12 months

Capital Bond Series "A"

Sold at £100 a unit from 4 January 1989 – 23 June 1990

Gross compound interest rate over 1st five years = 12.1%

Year	Annual gross interest £	Value anniversary of purchase £	Gross yield anniversary of purchase %	Net* yield anniversary of purchase %	Gross average yield to end term %	Net* average yield to end term %
1	5.50	105.50	5.5	4.1	12.1	9.1
2	8.97	114.47	8.5	6.4	13.8	10.4
3	13.16	127.63	11.5	8.6	15.5	11.6
4	18.51	146.14	14.5	10.9	17.6	13.2
5	30.10	176.24	20.6	15.5	20.6	15.5

Interest is added at the end of each 12 months

* After basic rate tax at 25%

Capital Bond Series "B"

Sold at £100 a unit from 24 June 1990 – 14 March 1991

Gross compound interest rate over 1st five years = 13.0%

Year	Annual gross interest £	Value anniversary of purchase £	Gross yield anniversary of purchase %	Net* yield anniversary of purchase %	Gross yield anniversary of purchase %	Net* yield anniversary of purchase %
1	8.50	108.50	8.5	6.4	13.0	9.5
2	11.12	119.62	10.25	7.7	14.2	10.6
3	14.95	134.57	12.5	9.4	15.5	11.6
4	20.52	155.09	15.25	11.4	17.0	12.6
5	29.16	184.25	18.8	14.1	18.8	14.1

Interest is added at the end of each 12 months

* After basic rate tax at 25%

Capital Bond Series "C"

Sold at £100 a unit from 2 April 1991

Gross compound interest rate over 1st five years = 11.5%

Year	Annual gross interest £	Value anniversary of purchase £	Gross yield anniversary of purchase %	Net* yield anniversary of purchase %	Gross yield anniversary of purchase %	Net* yield anniversary of purchase %
1	7.00	107.00	7.0	5.3	11.5	8.6
2	9.36	116.36	8.75	6.6	12.7	9.6
3	12.80	129.16	11.0	8.3	14.0	10.5
4	17.76	146.92	13.75	10.3	15.5	11.7
5	25.42	172.34	17.3	13.0	17.3	13.0

Interest is added at the end of each 12 months

* After basic rate tax at 25%

OLDER ISSUES OF NATIONAL SAVINGS CERTIFICATES

1st to 6th Issues

Sold between February 1916 and November 1939

Sell immediately. They yield between 1.2% and 2% a year.

Decimal, 7th, 8th, 9th, 10th, 11th, 12th, 14th, 16th, 18th, 19th, 21st, 23rd, 24th, 25th, 26th, 27th, 28th, 29th, 30th, 31st and 32nd

All units now earn variable interest every 3 months

There are no 13th, 15th, 17th, 20th and 22nd Issues

* General extension rate applies

APPENDIX TWO

General extension rates: interest variable

After the fixed term ends interest, at the GER, is added every three months, although interest is calculated monthly at the rate in force at the beginning of each month.

17 June 1982 to 30 November 1982 8.4%
1 December 1982 to 31 August 1983 7.08%
1 September 1983 to 31 March 1984 7.68%
1 April 1984 to 31 July 1984 6.84%
1 August 1984 to 30 November 1984 8.52%
1 December 1984 to 31 January 1985 8.28%
1 February 1985 to 31 March 1985 9%
1 April 1985 to 30 September 1985 9.51%
1 October 1985 8.52% to 31 October 1986 8.01%
1 November 1986 to 31 March 1987 8.7%
1 April 1987 to 31 April 1987 7.5%
1 May 1987 to 30 September 1987 7.02%
1 October 1987 to 29 February 1988 6.51%
1 March 1988 to 30 April 1988 5.76%
1 May 1988 5.01%

The current rate can be obtained at your local post office, by phoning 071-605 9461 or looking on Prestel page 5004213. The following Ansaphone numbers will also provide the current rate:
South – London – 071-605 9483/9484
North – Lytham St Anne's – 0253 723714
Scotland – Glasgow – 041-632 2766

APPENDIX THREE

The Retail Prices Index

The Retail Prices Index is the official measure of inflation or the cost of living. On the second Tuesday of each month about 300–400 employees from benefit offices around the country check the prices of over 600 goods and services purchased by typical families. These are collated by the Dcpartment of Employment and issued as an index number released on the second or third Friday of the following month. The index was re-based in January 1987 to take account of changes in our shopping habits, so all subsequent index numbers will appear lower than those listed opposite, which have not been adjusted for the change.

Index-Linked Savings Certificates

When you buy National Savings Index-Linked Certificates the index number which is used to work out the subsequent rise in the value of your certificates is the one for two months earlier. If you buy certificates in June, it is the April index number – which is published in May – which is the starting base.

When you encash your certificate, the same rules apply. The cash-in value of your certificates in June will relate to the April index-linked value, published in May.

On the Wednesday following publication of the RPI, *Money Mail* gives the latest value of certificates if they are sold the *next* month. As eight working days' notice is required, the following month is the earliest date at which the certificates can be encashed.

UK Retail Prices Index – 1914 to 1991

	1914	1915	1916	1917	1918	1919
Average	11.1	13.7	16.2	19.6	22.6	23.9
	1920	**1921**	**1922**	**1923**	**1924**	**1925**
Average	27.7	25.1	20.4	19.4	19.5	19.6
	1926	**1927**	**1928**	**1929**	**1930**	**1931**
Average	19.1	18.7	18.5	18.2	17.6	16.4
	1932	**1933**	**1934**	**1935**	**1936**	**1937**
Average	16.0	15.6	15.7	15.9	16.4	17.2
	1938	**1939–45**	**1946**	**1947**	**1948**	**1949**
Average	17.4	na	29.4	31.4	33.8	34.6
	1950	**1951**	**1952**	**1953**	**1954**	**1955**
Average	35.6	38.8	41.2	41.9	42.6	44.1
	1956	**1957**	**1958**	**1959**	**1960**	**1961**
Average	46.0	47.5	48.8	49.1	49.6	51.0
	1962	**1963**	**1964**	**1965**	**1966**	**1967**
Average	53.0	54.0	55.8	58.4	60.7	62.3
	1968	**1969**	**1970**	**1971**	**1972**	**1973**
Average	65.2	68.7	73.1	80.0	85.7	93.5
Jan			70.6	76.6	82.9	89.3
Feb	–	–	71.0	77.1	83.3	89.9
March			71.4	77.7	83.6	90.4
April			72.5	79.4	84.4	92.1
May	–	–	72.7	79.9	84.8	92.8
June			72.9	80.4	85.3	93.3
July			73.5	80.9	85.6	93.7
Aug	–	–	73.4	81.0	86.3	94.0
Sept			73.8	81.1	86.8	94.8
Oct			74.6	81.5	88.0	96.7
Nov	–	–	75.1	82.0	88.3	97.4
Dec			75.6	82.4	88.7	98.1

	1974	1975	1976	1977	1978	1979	1980	1981
Average	108.5	134.8	157.1	182.0	197.1	223.5	263.7	295.0
Jan	100.0	119.9	147.9	172.4	189.5	207.2	245.3	277.3
Feb	101.7	121.9	149.8	174.1	190.6	208.9	248.8	279.8
March	102.6	124.3	150.6	175.8	191.8	210.6	252.2	284.0
April	106.1	129.1	153.5	180.3	194.6	214.2	260.8	292.2
May	107.6	134.5	155.2	181.7	195.7	215.9	263.2	294.1
June	108.7	137.1	156.0	183.6	197.2	219.6	265.7	295.8
July	109.7	138.5	156.3	183.8	198.1	229.1	267.9	297.1
Aug	109.8	139.3	158.5	184.7	199.4	230.9	268.5	299.3
Sept	111.0	140.5	160.6	185.7	200.2	233.2	270.2	301.0
Oct	113.2	142.5	163.5	186.5	201.1	235.6	271.9	303.7
Nov	115.2	144.2	165.8	187.4	202.5	237.7	274.1	306.9
Dec	116.9	146.0	168.0	188.4	204.2	239.4	275.6	308.8

	1982	1983	1984	1985	1986	1987	1988	1989	1990	1991
Average	320.4	335.1	351.7	373.2	385.9	101.9	106.3	115.2	126.1	133.5
Jan	310.6	325.9	342.6	359.8	379.7	100.0	103.3	111.0	119.5	130.2
Feb	310.7	327.3	344.0	362.7	381.1	100.4	103.3	111.8	120.2	130.9
March	313.4	327.9	345.1	366.1	381.6	100.6	103.7	112.3	121.4	131.4
April	319.7	332.5	349.7	373.9	385.3	101.8	104.1	114.3	125.1	133.1
May	322.0	333.9	351.0	375.6	386.0	101.9	105.8	115.0	126.2	133.5
June	322.9	334.7	351.9	376.4	385.8	101.9	106.2	115.4	126.7	134.1
July	323.0	336.5	351.5	375.7	384.7	101.8	106.6	115.5	126.8	133.8
Aug	323.1	338.0	354.8	376.7	385.9	102.1	106.7	115.8	128.1	134.1
Sept	322.9	339.5	355.5	376.5	387.8	102.4	107.9	116.6	129.3	134.6
Oct	324.5	340.7	357.7	377.1	388.4	102.9	108.4	117.5	130.3	135.1
Nov	326.1	341.9	358.8	378.4	391.7	103.4	109.5	118.5	130.0	135.6
Dec	325.5	342.8	358.5	378.9	393.0	103.3	110.0	118.8	129.9	135.7

Index rebased January 1987 = 100. Divide "old" index numbers by 3.945 to convert to new base.

Source: Central Statistics Office. For later numbers phone 071-270 6363/6364

APPENDIX FOUR

CAR: The real rate of interest

The flat investment interest rates quoted by banks and building societies are sometimes followed by a slightly higher rate and the letters CAR. This stands for "compound annual rate".

If you reinvest your income in the same amount, rather than spend it, it can affect the real rate of interest you receive. Interest paid more frequently than once a year and reinvested itself begins to earn interest. And interest on interest adds up to a slightly higher interest rate than the flat quoted rate.

The compound effect of interest paid at intervals ranging from monthly to annually can add up to useful extra interest on larger investments, particularly when interest rates in general are high. If you spend your income, only the flat rate is relevant.

COMPOUNDED ANNUAL INTEREST RATES

Quoted rate* %	Compounded annual rate when interest is			
	Annually %	Half-yearly %	quarterly %	monthly %
5.00	5.00	5.06	5.09	5.12
5.50	5.50	5.58	5.61	5.64
6.00	6.00	6.09	6.14	6.17
6.50	6.50	6.61	6.66	6.70
7.00	7.00	7.12	7.19	7.23
7.50	7.50	7.64	7.71	7.76
8.00	8.00	8.16	8.24	8.30
8.50	8.50	8.68	8.77	8.84
9.00	9.00	9.20	9.31	9.38
9.50	9.50	9.73	9.84	9.92
10.00	10.00	10.25	10.38	10.47
10.50	10.50	10.78	10.92	11.02
11.00	11.00	11.30	11.46	11.57
11.50	11.50	11.83	12.01	12.13
12.00	12.00	12.36	12.55	12.68
12.50	12.50	12.89	13.10	13.24
13.00	13.00	13.42	13.65	13.80
13.50	13.50	13.96	14.20	14.37
14.00	14.00	14.49	14.75	14.93
14.50	14.50	15.03	15.31	15.50
15.00	15.00	15.56	15.87	16.08

* Net rate. Interest is taxable even if it is reinvested, so taxpayers cannot benefit in full from the compound gross interest.

INDEX

INDEX

INDEX

INDEX

INDEX